Creating your
own apothecary
is like cooking
food in your
own kitchen

From Earth

From
Earth

Create Your Own Natural Apothecary

CHARLOTTE RASMUSSEN

ROCKPOOL

This book is dedicated to my beautiful
husband and children. I am forever grateful
for the support and love they give me.

A Rockpool book
PO Box 252
Summer Hill
NSW 2130
Australia

rockpoolpublishing.com
Follow us! **f** ⃝ rockpoolpublishing
Tag your images with #rockpoolpublishing

ISBN: 9781925946253

Published in 2022, by Rockpool Publishing
Copyright text © Charlotte Rasmussen, 2022
Copyright images p. vi, 4, 6, 7, 8, 16, 19, 21, 24, 27-29, 31-32, 35-37, 39, 47-48,
90, 98, 101-105, 132, 134, 139, 140, 146-148, 150, 153-154, 159, 160, 165,
174-176, 178-180, 185, 187-188, 190-193, 195-196, 198, 200, 202
© Alexander Newbould (⃝ alexander_shore_photograpy), 2022
Cover image © Alexander Newbould, 2022

Other images from Shutterstock and Unsplash.

Copyright design © Rockpool Publishing, 2022

Design by Sara Lindberg, Rockpool Publishing
Edited by Rebecca Sutherland

 A catalogue record for this
book is available from the
National Library of Australia

Printed and bound in China
10 9 8 7 6 5 4 3 2 1

Contents

INTRODUCTION   1

INTRODUCTION TO YOUR NATURAL APOTHECARY AT HOME   17

UNDERSTAND NATURAL REMEDIES   33

QUICK GUIDE TO RELIEF   49

EASY AND QUICK GUIDE TO CREATING YOUR OWN BLENDS   91

SKIN AND HAIR CARE   99

REMEDIES   141

GENERAL HOUSE   177

ABOUT THE AUTHOR   197

RESOURCES   201

Introduction

From Earth is a book dedicated to my interpretation of a healthy lifestyle.

In today's world, we are constantly being overwhelmed by influencers, by ads that tell us what to buy and use and by unrealistic expectations of how we should look and what we should achieve in life. I look at my three children and hope as a mother that I will set a good example for them; most importantly by instilling the message that they can be themselves and feel good in their own skin.

The market is saturated with chemicals, preservatives and code numbers that most of us don't understand the meaning of – yet we are convinced through advertisements that we need these products in our life, even while not understanding the potential harm they could have in the long run or, frankly, what we are actually putting on our skin.

This book will help you understand your natural skin and hair health, as well as natural remedies that have been used for centuries. It is dedicated to those who want to go back to basics and remove unnatural and harmful ingredients from their life, by swapping to natural ingredients. I assure you that you will look and feel better than you ever have.

Have you always wanted to learn how to create your own natural skincare, remedies, or herbal teas? This book will show you the most simple and holistic ways of caring for yourself and your family by using natural ingredients such as oils, botanicals, essential oils, butters and more. It is as easy as any cooking recipe and you can follow the simple step-by-step instructions to start creating your own products from a beginner's level with ingredients that are safe to use.

This book is all about taking it back to basics, removing all the chemicals found in general skincare products and using simple but pure and natural ingredients to treat your skin, hair, and self. Within these pages you will find all the goodness nature has to offer and will learn about the natural benefits and properties found in various roots, flowers, herbs and more. You'll discover the incredible medicinal benefits of each individual ingredient used in the recipes and how to use botanicals to relive various complaints naturally.

You will also learn how to use carrier oils, essential oils, butters, dried flowers, herbs, roots and more to improve your health and wellbeing in a way that is in tune with the natural world.

Creating your own apothecary is like cooking food in your own kitchen; once you have a good idea of what the ingredients are and how you can blend them, you will quickly gain the confidence to go beyond these pages in creating your own combinations and recipes to suit your personal requirements.

Here, together, we are going to go back to the basics, cutting out the chemicals and artificial ingredients so commonly used in most products today. We'll learn about skincare, hair care, natural remedies, babies and children, products and lifestyle and how you can grow your own medicinal herbs from home.

The recipes are easy to read and understand and you will be able to customise your own handcrafted products exactly how you want with easy step-by-step guides. In return you will quickly find that your skin, hair and overall health will start glowing in response to these amazing ingredients that our planet has to offer, without the worry of the harm that artificial ingredients can have.

From professional surfers, to mums and busy bees working at the office, I have taught all kinds of people how they can benefit from the gifts provided by the earth; starting with very simple steps and with just a few ingredients, these friends of mine have flourished and – although not everyone ends up with a full garage of bottles like myself – they have

From Earth

found their own few favourite ingredients that they play around with and are proud to have full understanding and use of.

About From Earth

I love making the product. The benefits flow from the process. Form equals function, it's the Scandinavian way.

I grew up on a farm in Denmark where I played outdoors all day long, out running around in nature or riding my horse in the forest with my best friend. My parents worked many hours during the day so I was often left to my own devices, and I would spend hours roaming the acres I was growing up on, with an insatiable curiosity for plants that led me to spend hours picking leaves, berries and fruit.

At first, I didn't know much about plants. However, I found more inspiration in my grandparents' kitchen and their incredible basement. They had lived through the second world war, during which soldiers would take everything from them, so to survive they grew an abundance of food in their garden and then pickle and store it for winter. They would make their own wine from the berries and plants and catch fish from the lake between the mountains which they would store in their freezer so they could survive on their own.

On the mountain behind their house, they had a tiny little cubby house which I claimed as my own. My grandmother started teaching me about all the plants that she had in her garden and I would hang herbs to dry, blend them in oils and overall fall in love with natural ingredients.

Then, as teenagers do, I slowly started to focus on boys, music and make-up. I remember the other girls would tease me at school for having hairy eyebrows and hairy

legs, so to fit in I started plucking my eyebrows, shaving my legs, using make-up and following all the steps in the ads with shampoo, deodorant, moisturisers and so forth.

My skin quickly adapted to the moisturisers and especially lip balm; although I had never had an issue with dry skin or lips before, it was obvious that my skin had become 'addicted', so to speak, to the products I was using. Being a curious child, I wanted to know why.

I have a clear memory of adding moisturiser to water to see if I could blend the two. The result was not successful. I asked questions of how the products were made and what

From Earth

all the ingredients on the bottle meant, but no one was there to give me an answer; it was just something everyone used without knowing why they were doing it. My conclusion was that human beings would just do what everyone else was telling them, in person and in advertisements, to fit in.

Although my teenage armpits could not go without soap and deodorant, I generally stopped using the moisturisers and went easy on the make-up (unless there was a big party!).

I was always very true to myself while growing up. Many have commented on my skin and asked me what I use. My response is 'nothing', because I learned quickly that my skin, hair and so forth are better off without it and so much healthier.

By the time I moved to Australia, my roots of roaming in nature and going through the abundance of natural ingredients I found in my grandmother's basement had become a distant memory. I was married at the age of 22 and became a mother at 23. My obsession was always to be a good mother to my now three children, while I always kept myself busy with hobbies such as knitting, baking and painting.

I wanted to teach my children what I had been taught and, while creating candles and other items with a girlfriend, I slowly found my passion in plants again as well.

One product that I made was an oil for my daughter's eczema. This product worked so well that it was shared around in the community – it turned out that many struggled from eczema and were looking for natural alternatives. One product slowly became many through my passion and continued study, and it led to me finding that one thing I knew I wanted to do. From Earth was born.

Since then, it has had many ups and downs and bumps in the road. Any entrepreneur – especially someone who has never done it before – will tell you that there is much to learn on the way, but through my passion and determination it has become a successful company which now sells to shops across Australia and overseas.

Although I now have help in the manufacturing department, the recipes and ingredients are still the same. I feel blessed every morning waking up and being able to continue my journey by learning more about natural medicine and sharing it with my customers.

First Words

My mum simply did not believe in over-the-counter pharmaceuticals. If my siblings, friends or I got a rash, we would pick nettle leaves and scrunch them up (even if the rash was from running through a nettle field!). If we were sick, my grandmother would whip up soup or tea made with medicinal herbs. We learnt how to forage and enjoy the medicinal properties of the plants surrounding us, and how the earth could provide what we needed to be happy and healthy. This book is a tribute to my family and especially my grandparents, who live in Norway, and who taught me to live off the land we live on.

As you leaf through the pages of this book, I hope you will find inspiration to create your own natural apothecary by using botanicals, oils and essential oils to create the recipes that suit you and your family. This book is meant as a guide to storing and using medicinal plants in various ways for your health, and how not to waste anything from the garden. It is a fun and light book that anyone can learn from, with easy step-by-step instructions for beginners.

I believe that it is almost flabbergasting that we must teach around the subject of going natural – by which I mean using products without preservatives, chemicals, artificial ingredients and so forth. Somehow humans have evolved to allow marketing campaigns and advertisements an enormous amount of influence over what we put on our bodies, almost never questioning what chemicals are in what we are using; half the time these ingredient lists look like computer code that only a scientist would understand.

Growing up, I remember sneaking into my elder sister's room and trying out all the goods that she had stacked in her cupboard – as any young girl would do! But I was curious about how these things were made, asking 'how do they make body lotion? What are they putting in it?' Or, 'what makes it smell so nice?' I was the kind of child that loved asking questions, but typically I would be told not to worry about it. That was the kind of answer I hated the most.

I was not influenced by social media or advertisements when growing up; instead I was surrounded by farmland, animals and plants. I grew up picking berries every summer and going to Norway frequently to visit my grandparents, whom I adored. During the second world war they learnt to store everything and live in a very minimalistic way – and when I say minimalistic I don't mean that they had nothing. Their house was filled with treasures; with memories, a special scent and hidden gems such as hand-me-downs and homemade clothes. But my favourite was going downstairs into their cellar, which was always full! Homemade wine, frozen fish my grandfather had caught and shelves full of preserved food. They didn't ever buy much, or need much, and it has forever inspired me in life.

If as children we had a sore tummy, there were herbs to make us feel better; if we had a cold or a runny nose, there were even more herbs! If we had a rash on our skin it would be as simple as finding the right plant in our garden to scrunch up and use as a remedy.

So later on in life – when I started growing up and seeing what 'everybody else' was doing, including my sisters – I was of course fascinated, as any young girl would be, and for a while I was dragged into a world which I today perceive as fake.

There are so many advertisements now, attempting to convince you that you have to use a continual amount of five different products in your regular, or even daily, 'cleansing' facial routine. The extent that some brands or retailers will go to in order to make money can sometimes disgust me.

The worst one I ever saw was for a breast cream – made to massage onto your breast while checking if there are any lumps. The idea seems great, right? However, when looking closer I realised that the cream contained parabens; an ingredient that I distinctly remember having been shown to have possible links to breast cancer. I was horrified.

Another shock that I remember was when my firstborn child started developing eczema. When I took her to the doctor, I was prescribed a cream that they told me was under no circumstances allowed on her face. Imagine that? Using a cream on my baby's skin that was so harmful that she could not have it on her face!

I had a huge wakeup call and decided that for my children's sake I would venture back to my roots and find better alternatives.

This entire book is designed with that idea in mind. I don't want to talk too much about what chemical does what and what you should be avoiding. Instead I want to embrace a lifestyle in which you don't have to understand advanced chemistry to read the label on a product you might want to use, and I want to embrace a lifestyle where you know exactly what you are putting on your body. It should be almost basic knowledge for all of us to understand how to moisturise our skin, how to clean it and how to care for it, and I wish that it was also more commonplace to learn and know what the incredible plants in nature can do for you if you use them correctly.

This book is dedicated to all of you who ask questions. It is dedicated to those of you who have been through health scares, those of you who have families that you want to look after and those of you who just in general want to improve your overall wellbeing.

Many people advised me never to give my secrets away as they are also my business. However, if the will to do so is there, most of my secrets are out there to be discovered in books and webpages – after all, they are simple facts about the natural products of the earth and how they can be used. My passion has always been to educate people on the difference between what we *think* is real and what *is* real. And what is real is quite honestly so simple that everyone deserves to have that knowledge!

This book contains a huge amount of information about the ingredients I grew up surrounded by in my Scandinavian upbringing. I have also lived in Australia for a number of years now and, through asking lots of questions and researching because I am so passionate about plants especially, I have of course fallen in love with many of the incredible plants native to Australia. Wherever you are in the world there will be an array of wonderful, natural products to discover and add to your personal apothecary.

I love learning about and trying new ingredients and seeing what other countries and cultures have to offer, so I invite you to flip through these pages and learn more about the incredible benefits of our botanicals, and how to use them.

My Teachings

For me, it is not necessary to study something in school to gain knowledge and understanding. I follow my intuition in what I believe is right and wrong when it comes to skincare and remedies. When I started the process of creating my products, I received so many questions. These are some I would like to share with you along with my responses.

Why don't you make and sell 'normal' cream?

We need to start at the basics with this one. The pH balance of our skin is around 5.5 (4.5-6.5) and it makes sense to use products which are in the same balance as this. Our skin has a layer that naturally creates oil to keep our skin moisturised and protected, so in theory we should not *have* to moisturise, ever. From time to time, however, when seasons change and our skin can't keep up, or if we shave, or as our skin changes due to aging, we may have to give our skin a loving hand by adding natural oils to it (using oils which naturally have the same pH value as our skin).

The kind of cream that people generally buy in most stores is made by blending water, a wax substance and oil with a very strong preservative. Imagine you are cooking food – in most cases when you open a packet of food you have to use it within a few days or it will go rancid. Now with a cream, you are not just opening the packet – you are putting your fingers in it daily. So there must be enough preservatives in it to ensure that it still won't go rancid; in fact creams can last years, being used daily, even while being exposed to bacteria in the air and on your hands that would make the cream go bad without the preservative. To me, this is so unnatural and I don't understand why we do it, especially as the only beneficial part of the product is the actual oil and you can use that oil in its purest form without adding all the extra elements.

The other issues with commercially available creams is that the pH balance goes up to around 7-9, and due to the high water content it only moisturises your skin for a few hours, during which time your skin will start producing less natural oil – so you end up using your cream to unnaturally replace what was always there to help you in a more natural way. This is why I tell customers that you can not replace natural oils with creams. I'll discuss oils further, along with what I recommend for helping maintain healthy, balanced skin, in another chapter.

Why don't you shower everyday?

I have never been much of a shower person. Maybe I am lazy, maybe I don't really care – or maybe it is from my upbringing. I remember asking my grandfather how often he showered. He replied 'when I am dirty' (which for him was usually once a month). Don't get me wrong, it is not that I don't clean myself – I wash daily. Rather than a full body shower, however, I just wash the spots such as private areas and under my arms where I do need a clean every day. By only cleaning where I need to clean, when I need to clean, I have ended up having skin that never needs to be moisturised. I never break out with eczema (which I suffered with greatly when I was younger) or other skin concerns.

Here is the thing. As mentioned before, we all produce a natural oil in our skin which keeps our skin moisturised and protected. When we shower we are washing this natural oil off our bodies and it takes the skin 4-24 hours to replace the oils and restore the natural pH balance.

Humans did not always feel the need to bathe or shower daily – a wash cloth, water and ideally some soap was the best case scenario for clean hands, armpits and parts. Our skin must have loved us all back then! But then the bath tub was invented – and it seemed not to sell too well in the beginning. So the designer and creator (as the story goes) marketed this bath to rich people as something only people with money could have.

Soon enough the bath tub became a status symbol; only wealthy people could have a bath daily. And so a new habit was established. Then creams were produced, marketed in expensive jars, for wealthy people to moisturise their skin after each bath. If you think about it there was nothing natural about it!

I will not tell people not to shower daily – depending on the climate and how much exercise they're doing, many people just don't feel clean unless they have their shower. Most of my friends just love having a shower and will often do so daily as an indulgence. What I am saying is that showering every day will not benefit your skin in the longer run, so do ensure you use natural oils to help your skin with its natural oil production. And please be aware that if you suffer from eczema or psoriasis, less showering will allow your skin to heal much faster!

From Earth

What is your opinion on buying natural remedies at the pharmacy?

So remember how I spoke about creams earlier on? The same thing goes for all of these remedies that you can now buy for your skin. It may have that one magic natural ingredient in it, but it has most likely been diluted heavily with man-made chemicals (just read the ingredients on the back!).

If you really want to have your magic but want to have it naturally, it is by far the better option to actually buy that ingredient in whichever shape you can (herb, dried, oil or essential oil). I have seen many places in the world where the locals will treat a skin rash with leaves and flowers, then bandage it, and the next day it has disappeared like magic. The truth is it is not magic; we are just blessed to have so many beautiful botanicals that we can take advantage of that have incredible benefits for many things.

If you have aloe vera in your back yard you may already be taking advantage of its amazing gel after being sunburnt. This remedy is quite commonly understood, so why don't we understand and know what to do with all the other amazing plants? Using dried botanicals, for example, doesn't have to be complicated: you can simply put it in some olive oil as a natural preservative and use it on your skin, or use hot water to make a herbal tea. We'll discover some ingredients and recipes within the chapters of this book.

Why are all your products vegan and organic?

I am not strictly vegan in my diet, and I do not by any means only buy organic for myself, however I do believe that the more we do to limit the consumption of animal products and to move towards organic products, the more we move towards creating a healthier planet. To me going organic is of the utmost importance; the amount of chemicals sprayed on plants is killing all our natural wildlife in terms of insects, who create a better ecosystem. So, by purchasing organic products you are automatically cutting out the chemicals you are putting on your skin and in your body, and I believe that will make a huge difference..

Don't get me wrong – I love cutting a stem of aloe vera and rubbing it straight onto a sunburn! But many people don't realise that the gel you buy from the stores is filled with chemicals. Aloe vera goes rancid very quickly and does not keep its gel-like consistency for long without these chemicals. I encourage everyone to grow their own as it is so easy, however, if you are buying the gel, have a look at the ingredient label first so you at least know what you are using.

History and Evolution

I really enjoy the cultural diversity that exists on our planet, and the cultures I am the most interested in are those who still live the most in tune with the natural world; as some would say the most 'primitive'. I find it almost amusing that we as a 'more developed' class of society are able to judge and label so harshly, when I often find that those from whom I learn the most are those who come from long generations of continuing a very simple approach to life that does not revolve around money but has instead evolved around tradition and beliefs.

You may find surprising information and knowledge from your neighbour next door – I know I have on several occasions! But people who live very different lifestyles to my own, whose culture is based around survival, are those I often find the most inspiring. They understand living on Earth, living *from* the earth, and they know that you don't have to spend a huge amount of money on manufactured products when you can find the ingredients in nature for free.

I have met African tribal women who will teach you how to make moisturisers for your skin using shea butter from the tree nut, and how to get glowing skin by using turmeric. And I have found people in Asia who know exactly what to digest to help with gut inflammation. Meanwhile, someone takes these natural ideas into a more technologically developed society, concocts a product using those basic ingredients and markets it into products that we spend loads of money on because we either don't have those ingredients or because we just don't have the time to go harvesting and creating them ourselves.

Most of my own ideas came from my grandparents, and while I hope to inspire people around me to buy the basic ingredients and learn how to use them, there will always be someone too busy or not interested enough who will purchase them ready made instead – which is why I produce and sell my natural products.

I would be a fool if I for one second believed that I know or understand better than someone who has grown up in nature with no other resources than what they harvest and find – and therefore I would also be a fool if I did not carefully listen to what they have learned over thousands of years with information passed down through generations.

The magic that happens is when these traditions and beliefs are then studied using science and we can see how many of the ingredients used in traditional remedies and recipes have been proven to contain a naturally derived chemical that actually does help or give relief for what they have been used to treat. It blows my mind when I read through history how people discovered these benefits way before they were scientifically proven.

Introduction to your natural apothecary at home

A natural apothecary can vary from home to home; everyone's needs are different. For instance, I know women who have bad PMS, experiencing headaches and pain, and their apothecary would be filled with natural remedies to soothe these symptoms. Someone with young kids may have entirely different needs and have an apothecary filled with anti-bacterial sprays, mosquito and insect repellents or healing oils for rashes. This book will take you through many needs so that you can choose what is important to create and keep in your own natural apothecary.

What you need

EQUIPMENT

You don't need much to create your natural apothecary, but these are the items I always have handy when I start creating.

- Bottles and jars for the products. You can find varieties of glass bottles with pump, spray or dropper depending on what you are making, as well as glass jars with lids. My favourite go-to for all of these is Heirloom Body Care. Their details are included in my list of suppliers at the end of this book.
- Dropper measurement/pipette for essential oils.
- Measurement jugs.
- Scale.
- Cotton cloth or coffee filter for straining.
- Double boiler (or you can use two pots in the kitchen, one small placed in a larger pot).
- Jugs to pour (helps if there is a spout for easier pouring).

DRIED BOTANICALS

Example: Herbs, Flowers, Roots, Bark, Nuts, Leaves

Dried botanicals are great; they can be used in creating teas, used in cooking, or infused in oils. It is easy to end up stocking up on loads of these, and once you start creating it will become an addictive hobby (just look where it got me!). It is important to first understand the botanical you have foraged or purchased, what medicinal value it may have and what it can be used for. All of these will be explained in the next chapter.

CARRIER OILS

Example: Jojoba Oil, Almond Oil, Hemp Oil

Carrier oils are non-potent oils that are great to use straight out of the bottle. They can be used on your skin, for cooking and for infusions. Some carrier oils have a long shelf life while others don't; for example, olive oil and coconut oil will work as natural preservatives that will last for years, which makes them great for infusions. Oils such as primrose, on the other hand, may only last for 6 months.

Look for cold pressed oils! Oils can be pressed in many ways but when they are done by a heated process they often lose most of their natural vitamin and nutrition content. To find the best quality carrier oil, look for the words 'cold pressed' and 'organic'.

Carrier oils for your skin

Many worry that oils are too 'oily' and clogging, and in some cases, that is true. However, some oils are perfect for the skin. It all depends on the fat content of the oil; generally I use a scale of 1-5, with 1 being a dry oil that absorbs quickly and 5 being high in fat content and oily. These are my favourite oils and their scale of dry/oily.

Introduction to your natural apothecary at home

- ❧ Rosehip (1) Dry oil – Absorbs quickly.

- ❧ Jojoba (2) Dry/Medium oil, great as a moisturiser for the face especially.

- ❧ Almond (2/3) Medium and moisturising oil – great for the face.

- ❧ Hemp (3) A very healing and moisturising oil – use this when you need to repair and heal your skin.

- ❧ Coconut (5) An oil high in fat content and great for very dry skin as it is very moisturising. I do not recommend using this oil for eczema or psoriasis, or on the face by itself, as it may clog your pores and not allow the skin to breathe properly.

BUTTERS

Example: Shea Butter, Cacao Butter, Mango Butter

Butters are a solid form, derived from nuts mainly. Cacao butter is white and is used to create chocolate – mainly white chocolate, which is made with cacao butter and without cacao powder. All butters have great textures and are amazing in skincare products, for example in body butters. A body butter is created when you mix a butter with oil and whip it into a smooth and light cream. They have a ton of natural benefits for the skin and can be mixed with any essential oil into a cream that has the right usage for you. Be aware, though, that butters can be heavy and are not suitable for the face as they can be too clogging on the skin.

ESSENTIAL OILS

Example: Peppermint Oil, Tea Tree Oil, Lavender Oil

Essential oils are very potent oils that should always be handled with great care! There are a few things to look out for when purchasing an essential oil, particularly whether or not it is organic. So many oils on the market are filled with chemicals sprayed on the flowers before making them into essential oil, so for a good quality oil – go for organic! Also

check if your oil is 'pure'. Many essential oils now (and you will often notice this by the large difference in price) have already been diluted into a carrier oil; this gives you a less potent oil which you will end up using very quickly compared to a pure essential oil.

You need to dilute essential oils in a carrier oil or in water (be aware diluting essential oil in water will only last around 1-2 weeks in skincare or it will go rancid). The oil should be diluted using a maximum of 3% in the solution, due to its potency.

Essential oils are amazing because they contain so many nutrients and vitamins, they have great medicinal properties and can be used in so many varieties of ways. We'll be using essential oils in the recipes in this book.

HYDROSOL

Also referred to as … water! Hydrosols are created in the same process as when essential oils are created. Flowers are placed in a large container with water underneath to seep through the flowers and release the essential oils. The essential oil is very potent and comes out in little drops on the side, while the water which is left over is what we call hydrosol. Filled with the benefits of the flowers but in a much less potent dose, it can be used as is. It does not always smell as amazing as the essential oils, but is well worth using in face mists, toners, linen spray and cleaning products.

Introduction to your natural apothecary at home

OTHER

Natural Derived Vitamin E – Great to use as a natural preservative in oils to make your products last longer naturally!

Clay – Oh, how I love some wet dirt! Clays can be found naturally in so many places, from sea clay from the ocean to deep red clay from the desert of Australia. You will often find it in nature close to bodies of water, but to avoid the mess it is a lot easier to buy the clay as a dried powder. Dried clay powder comes in many variants; my favourites are kaolin, green clay, Moroccan Rhassoul clay, French pink clay and bentonite clay.

Salt – Bath salts, bath bombs (with salt), body scrubs, body scrub bars, face scrubs … I could go on. What would I do without the natural cleansing properties of salt? It's so easy to create your own products from this ingredient. You will be able to find it in fine, medium and coarse forms, to suit the level of exfoliation you are looking for. Be picky when choosing as there is a variety.

Diatomaceous Earth – A natural occurring algae fossil, made into a powder form. It is an extremely high absorbing powder which makes it great to use in masks or deodorants.

For a natural tonic, when you need a cleanse, just mix it with some water! I use it mostly when someone is feeling nauseas and coming down with gastro or food poisoning – it has saved me many times!

Candelilla Wax – A wax created from the flower. It's perfect to bind oils, creating a more solid form when melted together.

Examples of apothecaries

A BEGINNER'S APOTHECARY

I would recommend anyone stock these staples in their house and build on it to suit their needs. You can choose just one ingredient to get for your apothecary each month as you slowly replace pharmacy or skincare products while choosing a natural path. Essential oils may seem expensive at first, but you are only using small amounts at a time and they last a while, so you won't have to replace these often.

Containers

Amber bottles – 15ml, for essential oils.

Amber spray bottles – 100ml, for face toners.

Glass bottle with dropper – 30ml, for face oils.

Glass roll on bottles – 10ml, also known as lip gloss bottles.

Jars – any size, for balms, scrubs and body butters as well as teas.

Dried Botanicals

Peppermint – Use as a tea just as is for colds and headaches.

Nettle – Incredible for the gut when used in tea, but also a go-to if you have a rash or skin condition that needs to be treated. Just infuse in a carrier oil (read more on page 19).

Introduction to your natural apothecary at home

Lavender – Lavender is great for helping you to relax: in tea, in a bath or in a muslin bag stored under your pillow. May help with stress, headaches, and insomnia.

Carrier Oils

Jojoba – My favourite go-to oil! Use it on your face and body or infuse it with dried botanicals to create your own magnificent blend.

Coconut oil – Use it on dried or cracked skin, especially hands and feet.

Hemp oil – Use it to soothe your skin in case of rash, bites or other irritations.

Essential Oils

Lemon Myrtle – Blend 3% lemon myrtle essential oil in jojoba to use as an anti-bacterial relief for pimples, wounds, cuts, and bruises (*tip:* lemon myrtle has more anti-bacterial properties than tea tree). Also smells amazing when used in a diffuser.

Lavender – Use it in your bath or in a diffuser to help alleviate stress, soothe headaches and aid relaxation.

Chamomile – Chamomile might be costly, so it may not be the first thing you buy, but this powerful essential oil will heal any skin condition I swear! Blend it with jojoba or hemp oil and use it on scars, eczema, psoriasis, cuts, bites and more.

Citronella – Who doesn't have pesky mosquitos coming around every spring and summer? Use citronella in your carrier oil to create a natural repellent, or use in your diffuser to keep the bugs at bay.

Once you have your staple beginner's apothecary you can expand and follow some of my ideas here.

FAMILY'S APOTHECARY

With all of the things that our children go through, from bumps and bruises to runny noses and the occasional skin rash, you could be keeping a very large apothecary after a short time just to keep up with them. There are a few favourite ingredients that are definitely worth keeping on hand! I love castor oil for my children; it can be used on their red bums as a protective layer instead of Vaseline, which contains petroleum. I also use it on their noses when they go red.

The other thing I love is doing a blend of eucalyptus with peppermint essential oil. Make sure you only use 3% oil blended with jojoba and castor oil, then rub the solution on their chest or dab a tiny amount under their noses when a cold kicks in. Children also tend to love a warm bath with peppermint essential oil added as it gives them a refreshing scent, relaxes them, and helps with tension and headaches.

THE ATHLETE

Are you fit and sporty with the occasional sore muscles after a big work out? Camphor and wintergreen are two essential oils that are ideal for sore muscles. You can blend these with any carrier oil using 3% of the essential oil.

THE PREGNANT MUM TO BE

Pregnancy can be a tricky thing when trying to create your own natural products as many essential oils have not been marked safe for pregnancy due to not having been tested enough for side effects. I recommend trying to go essential oil free, except for lavender which is safe. Use the lavender essential oil to relax and pamper yourself as your body is going through big changes. Otherwise, if you must have essential oils, don't use them on your skin. Instead use them in your diffuser.

You can use pure hemp oil for stretch marks, it works an absolute treat!

MELANCHOLIC

I have friends, siblings and many acquaintances who are often tired, stressed, feeling anxious and sometimes depressed. Our hormones, diets and more can often play a large role in how we are feeling, but there are a few ingredients that will help relax you and improve your mood and overall health. Try creating a blend of lavender, patchouli and ylang ylang essential oils (1/3 of each) and use it in your bath and in your diffuser; you can also put a drop on your pillow before you go to bed. Even though you may not feel an immediate change, these essential oils have been studied and proven to help with stress and anxiety in particular and may be your remedy to calm your brain and relax your body.

If you have a tendency to get cold sores, another tip would be to use lemongrass to keep them at bay. Blend the essential oil as 3% of a solution with castor oil and use as a natural lip balm.

THE TEENAGER

So the hormones have kicked in? Your skin has started to break out? My best tip and advice is to always have activated coconut charcoal on hand (you can find my spot treatment recipe on page 111). Charcoal will absorb infections and when blended with clay it will dry up on the skin, taking the impurities with it. Also consider using lemon myrtle or tea tree to kill infection, while jojoba oil may help as a natural skin moisturiser that will create balance within your skin cells.

My apothecary ingredient list

It is important to mention that everyone keeps and stores different ingredients suitable to them – so know what you want and for what purpose you want to use it before going shopping. This list is just an example of what I like to keep stored.

Dried Botanicals
ALL organic:

- liquorice
- anise
- fennel
- chamomile
- lavender
- calendula
- nettle
- marshmallow root
- ginger

Introduction to your natural apothecary at home

- turmeric
- valerian root
- elderflower
- schisandra berries
- buchu leaf
- gotu kola
- chaste tree berries
- dandelion root
- cloves
- cardamom pods
- mulberries
- black haw
- rose petals

Oils and Carrier Oils
ALL organic:

- jojoba
- rosehip
- castor oil
- coconut oil
- hemp oil
- almond

From Earth

Butters
ALL organic:

- shea butter
- cocoa butter
- mango butter

Essential Oils
It is not always possible to find essential oils certified organic, but I always try and source these first:

- German chamomile
- eucalyptus
- ylang ylang
- rose geranium
- peppermint
- rosemary
- patchouli
- lemon
- sweet orange
- wintergreen
- camphor
- lemon myrtle
- lemongrass

Introduction to your natural apothecary at home

Clays

- red Australian clay
- green clay
- Bentonite clay
- kaolin clay
- pink French clay

Salt

- Epsom salt
- rock salt
- flossy sea salt
- fine sea salt

Hydrosol
ALL organic:

- lavender
- rose
- eucalyptus
- tea tree

Other

- Diatomaceous earth
- activated coconut charcoal
- natural derived vitamin E
- candelilla wax

Introduction to your natural apothecary at home

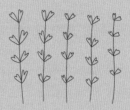

Understand natural remedies

The variety of natural remedies is so incredibly vast and there are so many plants out there with medicinal properties that it can be hard to figure out what to buy and use. To make it simple I'd like to share some of my favourite botanicals and explain their medicinal properties to show how they can be used and what you should potentially stock up in, in your own little kitchen! Please be aware that if you do have a medical history or are pregnant it is important to check with a medical professional or a naturopath before using these ingredients, as some may have side effects or may not have been tested enough to fully understand how it can affect a particular condition. One example which may be surprising is that chamomile has been linked to early labour. Ensure you have all the information you need before using any of these ingredients, and ensure you know how to take the right dose. And always bear in mind: everything in moderation!

LAVENDER

May help with insomnia, stress, anxiety, depression, tension, headaches.

I believe that most people will already know about this beautiful purple flower, which attracts bees in gardens found in most neighbourhoods. Lavender is very easy to grow and doesn't need much attention once established – I personally love growing it to pop in a vase, to use for smudge sticks or to dry the flowers and make a tea.

Forms: Flowers, hydrosol and essential oil.

Benefits: Lavender contains the compounds linalool and linalyl acetate, which are believed to reduce irritability and slow nerve impulses when absorbed through the skin or mucous membranes. This led to the theory and further research into the idea that lavender is helpful in treating stress, anxiety and insomnia.

Uses: Lavender can be used as its pure essential oil in spa and skincare products, diffusers and more; while its dried flowers can be used for infusions and teas.

Lavender is safe in pregnancy.

Recipes: Heat Pack (page 170), Sleep Better Tea (page 159), Face Mist (page 113), Sleep Mist (page 163), Relaxing Bath Salts (page 146), De-Stress Roll On (page 144), Smudge Stick (page 185)

MARSHMALLOW ROOT

May help with sore throat, or to soothe wounds and rashes due to anti-inflammatory properties.

Marshmallow root is not a plant you hear about too often. It is native to Europe and Western Asia. Centuries ago, it was used by the French to create soft lozenges called *pâté de guimauve*, which was used as a natural cough medicine and to soothe sore throats. Although marshmallow root is not commonly used in the actual marshmallows that we eat today, it was originally made by mixing its powdered form with water, which made it swell and thicken; then sugar was added and it turned into a sweet-tasting paste. The only thing the recipes have in common today is their sugar content.

Forms: Marshmallow root, marshmallow extract.

Benefits: The plant itself contains varying amounts of mucilage and pectin (mainly from the roots), which are believed to have strong soothing properties. It also contains compounds that are antiseptic and anti-inflammatory. The root of marshmallow is also known for its higher sugar content, which makes it sweet and perfect for teas.

Uses: Marshmallow root is mainly used dried in teas for sore throats and to create natural sweetness. It is also great to infuse in oils for its soothing properties.

Recipe: Natural Eczema Relief (page 150).

Understand natural remedies

CALENDULA

May help with soothing wounds and skin rashes, regenerating new skin cells, soothing tummy ulcers.

You might have seen this beautiful yellow-orange coloured flower in veggie beds around the neighbourhood. Also known as pot marigold and poet's marigold, it can be easily confused with the common marigold. It is easy to grow and harvest if you are up for some gardening, and its uses are many!

Forms: Flowers and extract.

Benefits: Calendula was originally used on the battlefield during the American Civil War, with the leaves used to help soothe burns, wounds and open sores. Back then physicians also used the plant to help treat conjunctivitis, stomach ulcers and liver complaints. Although further research into the plant is required, some studies have shown evidence of the herb stimulating the immune system, exhibiting antiviral action.

Uses: Dried flowers can be used in infusions of oil or as a tea.

Recipe: Natural Eczema Relief (page 150),Relaxing Bath Salts (page 146)

36

From Earth

CHAMOMILE

May help with eczema, sensitive skin, rashes, sore throats, tummy pain.

Growing up in Denmark, you could find chamomile everywhere during summer. It was a staple in our home if you got sick – I remember hating the taste of chamomile and honey that my mum would brew for me when I got a cough. As I grew up and started to study this little flower, it surprised me with its many and incredible benefits. The natural scent or flavour is not one that everyone will like – it is quite distinct – but it has become one of my go-to staples when creating skincare for sensitive skin and when making teas (I just add other herbs with flavours I find more pleasant to avoid the strong chamomile taste).

Benefits: There is a good reason why chamomile has the phrase in Germany 'capable of anything'! Chamomile has so many incredible benefits, including being anti-inflammatory, anti-bacterial, antifungal and antiseptic.

Form: Chamomile can be found as a dried flower that can be used in teas or for infusions, but it can also be found in its very potent (and expensive!) form of essential oil.

> Tip: *I find that the most beneficial chamomile essential oil is the German blue chamomile; it is very potent. When using the essential oil, you need to be careful with the amounts used.*

Uses: The essential oil can be used in skincare products and baths; when diluted in a carrier oil it creates a wonderful healing concoction.

Recipes: Healing Hemp Oil (page 95), Tummy Soother Tea (page 174)

37

NETTLE

May help with psoriasis, eczema, rash, irritated bowels, digestion.

I must admit I have a real soft spot for nettle! Some may find this confusing if they have ever had an encounter with the real 'stinging' nettle in the wild, as any skin that comes into contact with this plant will immediately develop a red, irritating and, in some cases, painful rash. But its ability to cause pain can also be reversed. Take the leaves, scrunch them up and apply to eczema, psoriasis or other skin rashes – even if the rash was because you got stung by the plant in the first place! You will soon see the amazing and immediate healing process. There is a certain technique to picking the leaves, if you are not wearing gloves, by picking them from the middle of the leaf and avoiding touching the pointy sides. I have used this plant and its leaves all through childhood and I swear by it!

Benefits: Nettle contains polysaccharides, which have been proven to show great anti-inflammatory effects. Nettle has also been shown to reduce pain in people experiencing rheumatic complaints.

Uses: The leaves can be picked (using gloves!) or you can purchase its dried leaves to use in teas and infusions.

Recipe: Natural Eczema Relief (page 150)

LIQUORICE ROOT

May help with stomach ache, liver damage, sore throats.

I have come to the realisation that not everyone in Australia is as big a fan of this wonderful root as we are in Europe – I feel like any child who has not had the experience of chewing on a dried liquorice root is missing out. It has its distinct liquorice flavour, which we are all familiar with, and a high natural sugar content that makes it sweet as it is, with no need to turn it into confection in my opinion. If you find it hard to chew the root as is, the next best thing would be to steep it in hot water as a tea and realise just how sweet and delicious it becomes!

Benefits: Liquorice contains saponin, which has been proven to show anti-inflammatory, antiviral and anti-arthritic properties. It is great for liver damage, stomach upsets and sore throats especially.

Uses: You can use the dried root in teas or infusions.

Recipe: Tummy Soother Tea (page 174)

Understand natural remedies

WINTERGREEN

May help with muscle pain, tension, arthritis.

Wintergreen is a scrub native to North America. If you ever come across a bottle of pure wintergreen essential oil and have a good sniff, you will immediately be transported to the football field and think of massages for muscle pain. Personally, I absolutely love the scent of wintergreen and I had to add it to my list. It is an absolute must have if you are into sports, suffer from arthritis or experience muscle pain and tension.

Benefits: Wintergreen contains methyl salicylate, an active ingredient which has anti-inflammatory properties and works as an aspirin-like compound. It is mainly used for inflammation and pain, which makes it especially good for arthritis and muscle pain.

Uses: The main use of wintergreen is from its essential oil, diluted in a carrier oil.

Recipe: Muscle Relaxant Body Butter (page 167)

HEMP

May help with rashes, sensitive skin, eczema, psoriasis.

Many people ask me in the store if I am legally ok to sell hemp oil. I can understand the question as it is often confused with cannabis. However, hemp oil is made from the seeds of the plant and does not contain THC (Tetra-hydro cannabinol), which is the active ingredient widely known to be illegal in many parts of the world. The oil derived from the seeds does have incredible benefits for your skin and can also be used in cooking, rather than olive oil to give an example, if you want to spice it up and try something different. When you find a good hemp oil (go for organic) it will have a deep green colour.

Benefits: Anti-inflammatory properties make it great for skin rashes or other inflammations when used in skincare products. More studies are still needed to fully research hemp oil and its benefits in terms of cooking and taking it digestively.

Uses: Hemp oil can be used as a carrier oil or for cooking. I love using it as a carrier oil and infusing it with other botanicals to create my own concoctions.

Recipe: Natural Eczema Relief (page 150)

41

JOJOBA

May help with dry skin and stretch marks.

I once read that jojoba has a similar extract to what we find in our breastmilk. It is known to be a soothing and protecting oil and, due to its lower fat content, it is amazing as a carrier oil that you can mix with essential oils to create your own concoction. It is one of my staple ingredients. It is grown in South America mainly, but also in Australia. The jojoba oil is derived from the seeds of its plant, making it more allergen friendly; so many oils are now made from nuts.

Benefits: Soothing and moisturising.

Uses: As a carrier oil you can use it in cooking and in skincare products – heck, you can even toss a little bit in the bath (just watch out as it may feel slippery afterwards). Your skin will feel silky smooth so it's worth the effort!

Recipe: Rejuvenating Face Oil (page 116)

From Earth

ROSEHIP (ALSO KNOWN AS DOG ROSE)

May help with regenerating new skin cells, stretch marks, fine lines and wrinkles.

You might be thinking, what is rosehip? But you would have come across it more than you might expect. Ever looked at a rose bush and wondered what the little red-looking berries are once the flowering has finished? Those are what you call rosehips. Rich in vitamins, rosehip oil is one of the only natural oils believed to help with regenerating new skin cells and therefore minimising fine lines and wrinkles.

Benefits: Rosehips contain a large amount of vitamin C but also A, B, E and K, making it a great oil for the skin and especially the face.

Uses: Use as a carrier oil and mix with other essential oils or another carrier oil to create your own concoctions.

Recipes: Pregnancy Body Oil (page 135), Rejuvenating Face Oil (page 116)

43

COCONUT

May help with dry skin, dry hair.

There are pros and cons to using this famous and delicious oil, which has gained a lot of popularity over the years. It has that natural, delightful scent that takes us all straight into a tropical fantasy on the beach, and we could probably all quite happily smother it all over ourselves! Use it in skincare products such as scrubs and body butters, or straight after shaving your legs, but be mindful when using it on your face as it has a high fat content and could be clogging your pores. And although coconut is great on the legs after a shave, please be mindful that it is not great on your private parts as it will not allow your skin to breathe.

Benefits: Coconut oil is filled with vitamins and is great for the skin and body, just be mindful that the internet can sometimes show an overwhelming amount of information that is not always correct. Coconut oil should never be used on eczema or psoriasis, despite the many articles surrounding this subject. I also highly recommend small doses if used on the face to minimise the amount of imperfections such as milia that could occur.

Uses: Use it for cooking or as a natural moisturiser.

Recipes: Muscle Relaxant Body Butter (page 167), Hair Treatment (page 130), Lush Body Butter (page 124), Firming and Exfoliating Body Scrub (page 121)

EUCALYPTUS

May help with bronchitis, sore throat.

It is easy to find eucalyptus around Australia, and its scent is well known to many. The uses are endless, from flower arrangements using its gorgeous leaves, to smudge sticks, to natural medicine treating coughs and colds through diffusers and natural oils.

Benefits: Eucalyptus contains cineole, which has antiseptic properties. The oil is great for creating your own natural vapour rub or for using in diffusers when you have a cold.

Caution: Eucalyptus oil can be toxic and should never be taken internally!

Uses: Eucalyptus can be infused using its leaves or you can purchase the pure essential oil.

Recipes: Vapour Roll On (page 157), Vapour Essential Oil (page 155)

LEMON MYRTLE

May help with wounds, cuts, infections, cold sores.

Lemon myrtle is an Australian native with an incredibly beautiful scent – sort of a mix between lemongrass and lemon, but with a very herbal effect. The essential oil derived from this plant has strong anti-bacterial properties, making this oil great to fight infections. It is one of my favourite ingredients for teenagers going through puberty due to its effectiveness in combating skin imperfections.

Benefits: Lemon myrtle's anti-bacterial properties may help kill infections and it can be applied to minor wounds, cuts and bruises. It can also be used when creating your own concoctions to fight pimples and acne. Lemon myrtle can also be a handy ingredient to create your own natural way of fighting cold sores.

Forms: Lemon myrtle can be found dried, but the most effective is the pure essential oil (which needs to be diluted).

Recipes: Natural Balancing & Anti-bacterial Face Oil (page 109), Natural Recipe Spot Treatment for Pimples (page 111), Natural Cold Sore Remedy (page 142)

Quick guide to relief

This is my go-to list when something pops up and I need my own natural relief. I mainly use the botanicals as tea, or I may use the essential oils mixed with a carrier oil. You can also try mixing and matching the different ingredients to make your own herbal tea.

Please note: It is important to read the information about uses and side effects included in this chapter, to ensure you are taking the botanicals in the correct way.

Complaints

STRESS

Stress is part of most people's lives; whether we are experiencing stress with finishing an exam, having lots on at work or going through emotional stress, most of us will experience stress from time to time. These are my suggestions to try and cope with stress better:

- ❧ Schisandra
- ❧ Ashwagandha
- ❧ Lemon balm
- ❧ Kava
- ❧ Valerian

ANXIETY

Anxiety can creep up on you when you least expect it and cause your heart to race and breathing issues. If you feel like you are suffering from anxiety often and severely, it may be worth speaking with a health professional. In the meantime, these botanicals are my suggestion as to what might help.

- ❧ Lavender
- ❧ Lemon balm
- ❧ Gotu kola
- ❧ Kava
- ❧ Liquorice
- ❧ Valerian
- ❧ Black haw

PRE-MENSTRUAL STRESS (PMS)

Many women suffer from particularly bad PMS symptoms, including nausea, sore breasts, bloating and pain. You can find medication over the counter, but many of these have an active ingredient that can actually be purchased and used as a natural product by itself. These are the remedies I suggest trying.

- ⚜ Chaste tree berries
- ⚜ Evening primrose
- ⚜ Red clover
- ⚜ Dong quai

DEPRESSION

An overwhelming amount of people are suffering from depression, an ailment that can make it hard to get up in the morning and go about your day as normal. If you are looking for a natural alternative to treat yourself for mild depressive episodes, these are the ingredients I suggest trying.

- ⚜ Lavender
- ⚜ Hemp
- ⚜ Black haw

HEADACHES

Headaches can come on for many different reasons and sometimes it is not noticeably clear why. There are some botanicals that have incredible benefits and target headaches. These are my go-to favourites.

- ❧ Lavender
- ❧ Peppermint
- ❧ Kava

MIGRAINES

When you get to the point where you can't stand any sound or light and all you can do is curl up into a ball in your bed with the lights off, you might be in for a rough time with a migraine. Luckily, some botanicals can work wonders on this, so if migraines are something you are prone to experiencing, these are the botanicals you should try.

- ❧ Butterbur
- ❧ Dong quai
- ❧ Feverfew

STOMACH CRAMPS

Stomach cramps can come out of nowhere and cause discomfort; you can feel bloated and in pain. If you don't know the cause of it, I would highly suggest that you seek professional advice as I lived with being an undiagnosed coeliac for much longer than I ever should have! Allergies, digestion issues, immune diseases and more are on the rise, so ensure you find the root of your issue! But if you need some quick relief and want to try something natural, these are my favourites.

- ᠅ Liquorice
- ᠅ Ginger
- ᠅ Marshmallow root

PERIOD CRAMPS

Period cramping can have a very distinct feeling and you know what is about to happen if it has not already started. If you are like me and the pain can be so intense that you are forced to lie on the couch, I highly recommend trying a heat pack and some of these botanicals.

- ᠅ Chaste tree
- ᠅ Dong quai
- ᠅ Black haw

OSTEOARTHRITIS

Although I do not have personal experience of osteoarthritis, I know that my dad suffers in intense pain with this. I started making him a body butter including wintergreen essential oil to help relieve some of his pain and it has since become one of his favourite products that I frequently have to send him in the mail. Go for these ingredients if you want to try and reduce the pain and inflammation.

- Devils claw
- Wintergreen

DIGESTION

If you suffer from heart burn, reflux or other digestion issues you should seek the advice of a medical professional first to ensure you do not have ulcers, allergies or other medical issues. But to relieve the symptoms of digestive problems, these are the ingredients to investigate and try out.

- Liquorice
- Ginger
- Lemon balm
- Catnip

RASH

Rashes can be caused by allergies, bites and more – I always go straight to this combo for immediate relief.

- ⚜ Hemp
- ⚜ Nettle

ECZEMA, PSORIASIS AND OTHER SKIN RASHES

I have always had eczema – it is not something that goes away unfortunately – but it can be managed very well, to the point that you rarely see it. Eczema can flare up due to allergies, diet, weather conditions, or even excessive washing or showering which may be stripping your skin of natural oils too quickly for its natural oil production to keep up. You likely will have met many with eczema on their hands since the onset of should this be written as 'COVID-19' ?-19 due to the extreme amount of handwashing and sanitising we have all been doing. Here are the best ingredients to try for quick relief.

- ⚜ Hemp
- ⚜ Nettle
- ⚜ Marshmallow root
- ⚜ Evening primrose

INSOMNIA

So you only had a few hours sleep last night and, although you have been up all day working and you can feel that your body and mind are tired, you are once again lying restless, tossing and turning in bed, desperate to get some sleep! Firstly, I hope that you have ensured you are not taking any caffeine or sugar before you go to bed. That aside, these ingredients may help you get some sleep.

- ❧ Lavender
- ❧ Catnip
- ❧ Hemp
- ❧ Valerian

MUSCLE PAIN

I must admit, I am not exactly sporty sporty, so I can't relate to those top athletes that need a good massage often to ensure their joints and muscles don't burst! These are some top natural medicinal remedies that will help with muscle pain, and I highly suggest trying them out.

- ❧ Wintergreen
- ❧ Feverfew
- ❧ Lavender

FUNGAL INFECTIONS

There are many different fungal infections we may experience. If you have been diagnosed with a fungal infection these are my go to ingredients to rub onto the affected area.

- ❧ Patchouli
- ❧ Eucalyptus
- ❧ Lemongrass
- ❧ Garlic

SEXUAL DISORDERS

There are many different reasons why men most typically go through sexual disorders, but women can experience them too. If you are genuinely concerned, always seek out a medical professional to ensure you know the cause of what is happening. If you are interested in trying some natural remedies to help with this, this is my list.

- ❧ Pygeum
- ❧ Chaste tree
- ❧ Marshmallow
- ❧ Ashwagandha

SORE THROAT

Wow, didn't COVID-19 really get us worrying when it came to a sore throat? Something that really is so normal to experience and that most people will be bothered by several times a year. There are always some great botanicals to keep in the cupboard to give you some relief.

- ❧ Ginger
- ❧ Eucalyptus
- ❧ Sage
- ❧ Seneca snakeroot
- ❧ Marshmallow

MENOPAUSE

The sweating, shaking, bloating and headaches might have started as you are about to go through this transition in life. Don't despair, there are some great natural remedies that will help you with all of these symptoms.

- ❧ Red Clover
- ❧ Chaste tree berries
- ❧ Dong quai

NAUSEA

Nausea can come on due to many different reasons. Typically the most common reasons to have nausea are from a good hangover or pregnancy. These two ingredients will sort you out!

- Ginger
- Peppermint

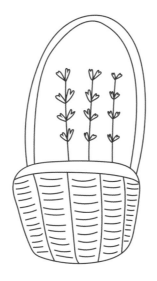

Remedies

SCHISANDRA

Schisandra has been proven through studies to increase a person's stamina and concentration while decreasing fatigue and recovery time. Other studies have pointed towards the berries also showing potential to work as an antidepressant.

Uses: The dried berries and leaves can be used to make a herbal tea.

Origin: China and Japan.

Warning: May cause heartburn in some cases.

60

From Earth

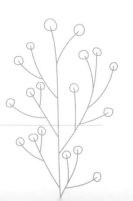

ASHWAGANDHA

Ashwagandha, also known as winter cherry, has shown powerful medicinal properties through studies. The plant has shown anti-inflammatory, sedative and immune-strengthening properties and helps with overall wellbeing. This plant may increase red blood cell count, strengthening the body as it goes through chemotherapy, leading to less side effects. It has also been shown to improve sexual performance significantly.

Uses: Roots, seeds and leaves can be used to make a herbal tea or eaten.

Origin: India, Africa, Mediterranean and Middle East.

Warning: Ashwagandha should not be taken during pregnancy or taken with alcohol, medication or other sedatives.

LEMON BALM

Research has shown that lemon balm has calming effects on the central nervous system. When used together with valerian root it has also been shown to be very effective for insomnia and anxiety – studies showed more improvement for those taking this blend than those given a placebo.

Uses: Leaves can be used in cooking or dried and used as a herbal tea.

Origin: Southern Europe and Western Asia.

Warning: Lemon balm is not linked to any side effects or symptoms, however it is strongly recommended that pregnant women and breastfeeding mothers do not use lemon balm as further research is required to determine whether it is safe.

KAVA

Kava has shown strong medicinal properties which are sedative and muscle relaxant. It has also shown efficiency in treatments of tension, anxiety and agitation due to kavalactones, the chemically active compound found in kava, which binds itself to various neuroreceptors in the brain, including the dopamine receptors.

Uses: Underground stem and roots. Can be made into a drink – although be aware, it may be bitter.

Origin: Polynesia.

Warning: Kava should not be taken in large doses as it can affect the liver if taken daily over a longer period. Kava is not recommended for pregnant or breastfeeding women.

VALERIAN

Valerian root has been a go-to for many people who are experiencing insomnia as it has been proven to improve overall sleep quality and help those who are experiencing insomnia. It may also help with relaxation as it works as a natural sedative. Personally I know many who do not like the taste of valerian root! I highly recommend trying to blend your own chai and drink it nightly before going to sleep, or try my sleep better tea (see recipe on page 159).

Uses: Root can be made into a tea.

Origin: Native to Europe and Asia.

Warning: Valerian root has not shown any side effects and is considered safe even with alcohol.

64

LAVENDER

Lavender is proven to help relax your mind because it contains the compounds linalool and linalyl acetate, which are absorbed through the skin or mucous membranes. These help depress the central nervous system by slowing nerve impulses while reducing irritability and pain.

Uses: Flowers can be used, or use as an essential oil. Blend 3% lavender essential oil with any carrier oil before using on the skin.

Origin: Mediterranean.

Warning: There are no known side effects to using lavender and it is considered safe even in pregnancy.

GOTU KOLA

Gotu kola has been confirmed to work as a natural sedative with anti-inflammatory effects and is also proven to stimulate the production of collagen helping with wound healing as well as positive effects on cells and tissues

Uses: Leaves and stems can be eaten or used as a herbal tea.

Origin: Native to Asia, Africa and Madagascar.

Warning: There are no proven side effects and gotu kola is considered safe.

LIQUORICE

Liquorice is a well-known root used in many sweet treats. I was one of many children growing up chewing on the root itself as it has a sweet natural flavour. Liquorice has strong anti-inflammatory and anti-arthritic properties and it stimulates the immune system. It also helps people who have diabetes as it helps to prevent build-up of the sugar sorbitol in the body, which also helps the health of kidneys, vision and ulcers. Liquorice is also commonly used in cough medicine.

Uses: The underground stem/root. Liquorice is delicious when eaten dried and raw, but is also amazing when brewed up as a tea.

Origin: South of Europe and Central Asia.

Warning: Excessive and prolonged use of liquorice can lead to high blood pressure and water retention.

67

CHASTE TREE BERRIES

Chaste tree berries are a godsend for women! They help stimulate the production of progesterone in the second half of the menstrual cycle, which balances out the hormones that regulate fertility, menstruation and other processes. This eases the symptoms of PMS such as bloating, mood swings, anxiety, headaches and breast tenderness.

Uses: The fruit can often be found dried. It can be eaten or used in herbal teas.

Origin: Southern Europe, the Mediterranean and Western Asia.

Warning: Chaste tree berries should not be taken during pregnancy or fertility treatments.

68

EVENING PRIMROSE

Evening primrose is known to assist with hormone production and has shown some signs of giving relief in premenstrual symptoms, although further studies are needed. Another benefit of primrose is that it has been reported to have significant success in treating conditions such as eczema.

Uses: As a seed oil can be rubbed on eczema, used as a carrier oil or rubbed on the belly during PMS.

Origin: North America.

Warning: There are no reported side effects of evening primrose.

RED CLOVER

Red clover contains the active ingredient isoflavones, which help relieve the symptoms of PMS and hot flashes. Use of red clover also causes a high increase in the elasticity of the arteries, which may assist in reducing the risk of cardiovascular disease, which has been associated with menopause.

Uses: Leaves and flowers can be found dried and used as a tonic or in herbal teas.

Origin: The east Mediterranean and Asia.

Warning: There are no reported side effects of red clover.

70

From Earth

DONG QUAI

Containing phytoestrogens and coumarins, dong quai has shown to improve levels of estrogen when they are naturally low in women, which may help ease the symptoms of menopausal and postmenopausal women. Dong quai also shows benefits in tissue cramping and migraines, and in some studies has proven better at relieving pain than aspirin.

Uses: Roots are often found dried and must be mixed with hot water to release the phytoestrogens and coumarins.

Origin: China, Korea and Japan.

Warning: Dong quai should only be taken in small doses and not consistently. Dong quai should not be taken during pregnancy, breastfeeding or fertility treatment.

BLACK HAW

The main chemical components in black haw are scopoletin and aesculetin, which benefit muscle contractions and relieve pain as they have a sedative effect on the uterus. These components have also shown benefits when treating anxiety and depression. Black haw also has anti-bacterial agents as well as anti-inflammatory properties, which have been used to treat bronchial conditions such as asthma.

Uses: The bark can be found dried and used as a tonic by adding 1 teaspoon to a pot of hot water.

Origin: United States.

Warning: Black haw should not be taken by anyone who has an aspirin allergy. Other side effects reported are nausea and intestinal discomfort.

72

From Earth

HEMP

Hemp has many incredible benefits and is known mostly to have sedative and relaxing effects. Personally, I have seen many benefits of using hemp oil on various skin conditions such as eczema and psoriasis. When purchased as an oil it is made from seeds, making it legal to use in most countries and very accessible.

Uses: Hemp seed oil can be used directly on the skin or blended with 3% essential oils.

Origin: Western and Central Asia, Northern India and South of Siberia.

Warning: Hemp leaves and hemp seeds are two very different things and, although I would love to see hemp oil made from leaves legalised as it has so many incredible benefits, we must wait as the leaves contain cannabis and are therefore considered illegal in most countries. Until then you can enjoy the benefits of hemp seed oil, which can be purchased in most health food stores. This oil has been shown to be very safe to use.

73

PEPPERMINT

Peppermint's main beneficial ingredient is menthol, which helps calm the stomach, reducing bloating and improving digestion. Peppermint has also been shown as beneficial to cold receptors in the nose and throat, and is an effective decongestant when you have a cold. When used as an essential oil and rubbed on the forehead and temples it can provide relief from headaches.

Uses: Peppermint can be used in cooking, as a herbal tea using the leaves fresh or dried, or it can be used as an essential oil – only use 3% blended with a carrier oil, then rub into the chest and around the nose for a cold, or on your temples and forehead to reduce the symptoms of a headache.

Origin: Europe and Asia.

Warning: Peppermint may cause heartburn and indigestion in those who have GERD (gastroesophageal reflux disease).

74

BUTTERBUR

An incredible study on butterbur showed that it reduced the frequency of migraine attacks as well as pain and duration by 60% (compared to those using a placebo). The main therapeutic ingredients of butterbur are petasin and isopetasin, which have been shown to help reduce muscle spasms in the walls of blood vessels in particular. Butterbur also shows anti-inflammatory effects and has been used treating bronchial spasms in asthma patients.

Uses: Leaves can be purchased dried and made into a tea.

Origin: Europe and northwest Asia.

Warning: There are no reported side effects found with butterbur.

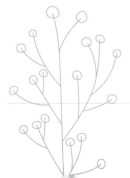

75

GINGER

What a wonder ginger is! It has so many medicinal benefits and is one of the easiest rhizomes (underground stems) to find, accessible to us all in supermarkets. Ginger contains the chemicals known as gingerols and shogaols, which work as natural anti-inflammatories that help settle stomachs by encouraging contractions that move food through our digestive tract. Ginger also has extraordinarily strong antinausea effects that may help reduce motion sickness and ease the nausea associated with pregnancy. Furthermore, ginger has also been shown to potentially lower cholesterol and prevent the platelet aggregation that can lead to blood clots.

Uses: Used fresh in cooking and teas or dried as a powder. You can also purchase ginger as an essential oil, although this should not be digested and is mainly used for its scent blended with other essential oils.

Origin: Tropical Asia.

Warning: There are no reported side effects to using ginger.

MARSHMALLOW

Marshmallow root was originally used when making marshmallows, however the plant is not used for this anymore. Instead it is often used as a cough medication as it has anti-inflammatory and soothing properties. Personally I have also used marshmallow root infused in oils, as I find that it works wonderfully in soothing the skin due to its anti-inflammatory properties. It is great when treating eczema or psoriasis.

Uses: The roots, leaves and flowers of the plant can be used. I mainly use the root to create teas that are great for sore throats, or I infuse it in carrier oils to be used on the skin.

Origin: Europe and western Asia.

Warning: There are no found side effects to using marshmallow.

PATCHOULI

Although patchouli is still being studied, it has shown suggestions of anti-fungal and anti-bacterial effects in an Indian study, where it was effective in all the fungi tests and the majority of the bacterial tests. Patchouli can be used blended with a carrier oil to help skin fungal infections.

Uses: Blend 3% of pure patchouli essential oil with a carrier oil and use on the skin where a fungal or bacterial infection may be present.

Origin: Indonesia, Malaysia, China, Brazil and India.

Warning: Patchouli should not be taken internally.

DEVIL'S CLAW

Devil's claw contains a high level of iridoid glycosides compounds which have shown anti-inflammatory and analgesic effects. These extracts reduce pain from osteoarthritis just as effectively as any of the brand-name drugs you might buy at the chemist. Devil's claw is reported to reduce pain and inflammation when taken daily.

Uses: The secondary roots of this plant can be used as a tonic when blended with hot water or mixed in with a herbal tea.

Origin: Africa.

Warning: There are no reported side effects or warnings in regard to using devil's claw, although more research is needed as it has not been extensively studied.

CATNIP

Catnip is known mostly by the effect it has on cats, as they are drawn to it and show a significant happiness and drowsiness around the plant, which can be quite amusing for the human spectator. Catnip is in fact an incredible plant with many medicinal properties. Its main active ingredient, found in the oil, is a chemical called nepetalactone. This extract has calming effects and can be soothing when taken digestively as a tea as it may help relieve gas and bloating.

Uses: Leaves and flowers can be found fresh or dried. Catnip can also be found as an essential oil and, blended with a carrier oil, it would have soothing properties on the skin.

Origin: Europe and Asia.

Warning: There are no reported side effects for catnip.

STINGING NETTLE

I have mentioned it before and I will do it again, this plant is just a wonder! And although it can sting it belongs in any household apothecary in my books!

Nettle contains polysaccharides, which have strong anti-inflammatory properties, and is well suited for using in skincare and in herbal teas. As children, we would pick the leaves from the centre (avoiding touching the outer leaves) and scrunch them up into a ball to apply to mosquito bites, stings and other skin conditions, which gave us immediate relief.

Uses: Fresh leaves or dried leaves can be added to an oil for skincare. Dried leaves can also be used as a tea.

Origin: Europe and parts of Asia.

Warning: There are no reported side effects of stinging nettle.

WINTERGREEN

Wintergreen contains high levels of methyl salicylate, which is found in the essential oil derived from its leaves. This compound has shown to be even more effective than aspirin and with less side effects, making it a beneficial anti-inflammatory oil that helps with pain relief. I use it often in skincare products when my clients have arthritis or muscle pain, and it has worked wonderfully.

Uses: The leaves are made into essential oil. Always dilute only using 3% of the oil blended with a carrier oil, then massage into skin and muscles to relieve aches and pains.

Origin: North America.

Warning: Wintergreen should only be used on the skin as it is very toxic if taken internally. Always dilute with a carrier oil. If you have an aspirin allergy, it is not recommended to use wintergreen.

FEVERFEW

Feverfew contains camphor, a chemical compound that helps inhibit smooth muscle contractions, which may help with muscle pain and migraines. It is also known to be anti-inflammatory. It can be taken as a tea or you can buy the compound camphor in an essential oil to use on sore muscles and arthritis, although more studies are needed to confirm if it has positive effects on the latter.

Uses: Leaves and flowering tops can be made into a tea. Camphor, the main compound, can also be purchased as an essential oil and diluted with a carrier oil to use on the skin.

Origin: Europe.

Warning: Some individuals have reported getting mouth ulcers after chewing on the leaves or drinking tea made from feverfew. If you purchase camphor as an essential oil this should never be taken orally and should only be used on the skin once blended with a carrier oil, with the essential oil as 3% of the solution.

EUCALYPTUS

Eucalyptus is a classic medicine in Australia, as I have learnt since moving here. The oil derived from the leaves has an active ingredient called cineole, which has antiseptic properties. The oil can be used to help dilate the bronchioles in the lungs to make it easier to breathe. It can also be useful in treating ear infections, cuts and bruises.

Uses: Essential oil from the leaves can be blended with a carrier oil then rubbed into the chest and around the nose as a decongestant. You can also use the essential oil in a diffuser or hot steam to ease congestion and relieve cold symptoms. The leaves can be used to brew tea.

Origin: Australia.

Warning: Eucalyptus oil should never be taken orally and needs to be diluted with a carrier oil as it is otherwise toxic. Even diluted in a carrier oil, be sure to avoid the eye area.

From Earth

LEMONGRASS

One of my favourite scents, lemongrass has delightful citrus and herbal notes to it. Lemongrass also has significant antiseptic, anti-bacterial and anti-fungal properties, making it an ideal oil to keep in your apothecary. It can be used diluted with a carrier oil on cuts and bruises as well as cold sores and fungal infections such as athlete's foot and ringworm.

Uses: Essential oil is derived from the leaves and young stems. It needs to be diluted using 3% in a carrier oil, after which it can be applied to any affected area.

Origin: India and Sri Lanka.

Warning: Lemongrass oil can be toxic and should never be ingested. When used on the skin it should always be diluted into a carrier oil first.

GARLIC

Found in most kitchens, garlic is versatile and delicious when used in cooking. But many don't know that garlic also has very notable antibiotic, antifungal and antiviral properties from the allicin which is created when you crush a garlic clove. Garlic has also shown an ability to reduce the likelihood of blood clots and remove plaque from the blood vessels.

Uses: The garlic bulb is separated into cloves, which are then crushed for the best medicinal properties. Garlic can be used in cooking but can also be rubbed straight onto a fungal disease.

Origin: Central Asia.

Warning: No side effects have been found to using garlic.

PYGEUM

Triterpenes is the active ingredient found in pygeum; this has anti-inflammatory effects and compounds that help prevent cholesterol build-up. Pygeum is also used in treating male sexual dysfunction as well as infections in the prostate and seminal vesicles. Other studies have also shown that it may be used to help increase hair growth, semen viability and to treat urinary tract infections.

Uses: Bark, leaves and fruit can be digested or bought dried for tea.

Origin: South Africa and Madagascar.

Warning: Pygeum should not be taken if a test to rule out prostate cancer has not been done first. Some side effects include mild gastrointestinal distress. It is not recommended to be used by pregnant or breastfeeding women or by children as there has not been sufficient research carried out yet.

SAGE

Sage has shown superb medicinal benefits in being antifungal, anti-bacterial and antiviral, and it has astringent properties. It is a great herb as it is easy to grow in your herb garden or access in a supermarket. Sage can also be purchased as an essential oil and blended with a carrier oil to use directly on the skin for any fungal diseases or on cuts and bruises.

Uses: Leaves or essential oil.

Origin: The Mediterranean.

Warning: Sage should not be taken by breastfeeding mums as it may lower the milk supply. Sage essential oil should not be used during pregnancy either, however it is safe in foods.

SENECA SNAKEROOT

Seneca snakeroot is used widely in Europe in cough medicine as it contains the compound triterpenoid saponins, which has anti-inflammatory properties, helps control coughing and is mucus-thinning. The plant has also been shown in studies to cause a coughing reflex, helping to clear infection from throat and lungs, and induce sweating, which can help break a fever.

Uses: Roots can be brewed into a tea.

Origin: North America.

Warning: Side effects of Seneca include nausea and if large doses are taken it can cause vomiting and diarrhea. Only small amounts should be taken to treat a sore throat or a cold. Take care due to the aforementioned effects of coughing and fever.

89

Easy and quick guide to creating your own blends

Essential oil can be divided into seven categories (see pages 92-93). There is a lot to take onboard when starting out, and it can be tricky in the beginning to figure out what matches well. This is a foolproof guide to show you what you can start blending. Once you have given it a good crack you might try to mix and match outside of the 'wheel' pictured, but this is the easiest way to start out.

Essential oil should always be diluted, whether you are using it in a bath, a diffuser, in skincare or blended with a carrier oil with 3% essential oil to 97% carrier.

It is also worth noting that most essential oils are not safe to use when pregnant.

Floral

Examples of the Floral type are:

Chamomile, Rose Geranium, Lavender, Jasmine and Rose.

Resin

Examples of the Resin type are:

Frankincense, Myrrh, Camphor, Vanilla and Benzoin.

Exotic

Examples of the Exotic type are:

Patchouli, Sandalwood, Vetiver and Ylang Ylang.

Spice

Examples of the Spice type are:

Bay leaf, Cardamom, Aniseed, Ginger, Nutmeg, Clove and Cinnamon.

From Earth

Wood

Examples of the Wood type are:

Eucalyptus, Juniper, Pine, Tea Tree, Juniper, Lemon Myrtle and Cedarwood.

Citrus

Examples of the Citrus type are:

Sweet orange, Mandarin, Lemon, Lime, Lemongrass, Grapefruit and Tangerine.

Herbal

Examples of the Herbal type are:

Basil, Clary Sage, Marjoram, Peppermint, Thyme and Rosemary.

Easy and quick guide to creating your own blends

Creating Your Oil For Skincare and Remedies

When starting out and wanting to create your own blends that are safe to use directly on your skin, you can be quite creative. This is my step-by-step guide.

STEP 1

Choose a carrier oil (page 28) or more than one carrier oil to create a base for your oil.

Example: Hemp oil – Anti-inflammatory.

STEP 2 (OPTIONAL)

Choose an infusion, or more than one, by choosing from the botanical list (pages 27-28) something with some of the relief symptoms that you are looking for.

Example: Chamomile – Soothing.

Add the herbs to your oil and let it sit for a week to infuse in a dark and cool place.

Once it has been sitting for at least a week, strain using a coffee filter or a muslin cloth.

95

STEP 3

Add your choice of essential oil. This can be as a preferred fragrance or to further enhance the medicinal properties of your oil.

Example: Lemon Myrtle – Anti-bacterial.

STEP 4 (OPTIONAL)

If you want your oil to last longer (up to two years), add a drop of naturally derived vitamin E.

Note: *It is easy to know if your oil has gone rancid as it will generally start creating a bad odour – so you can always give it a sniff to see if it still smells good. An oil blend like this should last several months and if you use the naturally derived vitamin E it should last up to 2 years.*

From Earth

Creating your own tea blend

Teas can be made by creating your own blends from dried botanicals – just ensure that you know what to use and what it is for. For example, St. John's wort can be fatal for pregnancies but has incredible benefits towards depression, insomnia and concentration. It is important to always look up side effects before mixing if you are unsure.

Creating your own face mist

Hydrosols are amazing! Hydrosols are basically the water content left over during the process of creating an essential oil. So the water can be infused with lavender, rose, chamomile, myrtle, eucalyptus and more. It does not smell as strong as an essential oil but it has many benefits from the botanical used. They are also more affordable and less harsh.

If you want to create a face toner you can use any chosen hydrosol and blend it 50/50 with witch hazel (water based).

Note: You can mix any hydrosol together to create your own face mist blend, but never mix it with an oil base as it will go rancid.

Easy and quick guide to creating your own blends

Skin and hair care

Face, body and hair

We must be completely re-educated when it comes to our skin. Essentially your skin knows how to look after itself without the use of any products, just like all animals on our planet! But it is nice to spoil ourselves and many plants offer amazing remedies to improve our skin and hair health – so we might as well take advantage of it.

My biggest concern with the skincare products found in shops is that it is often hard to even understand the ingredients used in these products as they are made up of so many man-made chemicals and a very small amount of natural ingredients. In my opinion, it should be all natural ingredients and labels should be easy to read and understand. Next time you pick a product up, try and read through the ingredients list and take note of the first few ingredients mentioned as they will be the main component in the product. Be aware of what you are using on your skin and hair as it may feel great at the beginning but won't benefit you in the long run.

ORGANIC VS NATURAL (OR BOTH!)

I remember having this discussion with a friend: what is more important? Whether a product is organic, or whether it is natural? She was convinced that you should always go for a product marked organic first and that it was the most important thing. This begged me to ask the question, are people actually aware of what is inside the products they are buying, or do they just read the front label?

Organic

Organic basically means that the main ingredients used in the products have not been sprayed with chemicals during the process. For example, if you buy an organic hemp oil it means that the plant has not been sprayed for pesticides while being grown, which is overall better for nature and our planet.

Organic products can be made with chemicals that are not classified as organic, it is like the blacklist of ingredients which are not counted as a percentage of the whole because they may work as a preservative or other function that certifications don't count in. I have found several products that were marked as organic, but when I read through the ingredients label I quickly discovered that the product was mainly made up of chemicals and only a few organic ingredients had been added. So next time you go shopping, don't just check the organic certification; check the ingredients, ensure that you understand what they are and what they are for. Anything that contains SLS, PEG numbers or parabens I would always stay clear because they have been linked to causing health issues.

Natural

A natural product is made up of at least 95% natural ingredients. You will generally discover when reading the ingredient list that the product has been made from ingredients that you will most likely know. A natural product does not however mean that it is organic. It is like buying an apple from the supermarket; it may have been sprayed with chemicals, but it is still a natural product.

Go For Both

The ultimate product for me personally is a product that has been marked natural *and* organic. If you understand the ingredients and what they are, and the product has been marked organic, you are on to a winner!

Skin and hair care

PH BALANCE & OIL PRODUCTION

Our skin likes a pH balance between 3.5 and 5.5. Generally oils are naturally in this range and work as natural moisturisers and protection for our skin while being 100% natural.

Water, however, has a pH level of 7. When we shower or have a bath, we wash off the natural oils created by our skin to protect and keep us moisturised. If you shower every day it is more likely that you have either dry skin, due to your natural oil production not being able to create enough oil to keep your skin moisturised, or you may experience having oily skin due to your skin going into overdrive and producing too much oil. The same thing goes for your face and for your hair (ever noticed that your hair becomes oily after a day or two without washing if you normally wash it every day?).

In Scandinavia, my grandfather (who always looked incredible by the way) never seemed to shower – he would say 'I shower when I am dirty'. It made me laugh, sure, but it also makes so much sense to me. Generally you will find many people in Norway, instead of a daily shower, will just use a wash cloth to wash their 'dirty' parts, under their arms and so on, while leaving the rest of the skin alone.

SUN

We all know that too much sun is damaging for the skin and over time will make your skin look and feel leathery. I never used to have this issue as the sun is a rare thing in Scandinavia compared to Australia. When the sun came out in Norway we were all out and about trying to get as much sun as possible! But Australia, oh so different – in Australia really you want to stay away from the sun due to how much harsher it is on the skin. I know many Danish people who have said 'oh I'll be fine' and after 30 minutes in the Australian sunshine they come back red as a tomato! That said, wherever you are you should be careful to protect your skin, because even when it does not feel harsh it can be harmful.

If you want, you can make a natural sunscreen using zinc and water or oil, however, a completely natural sunscreen made this way will make you look white compared to sunscreens sold in the shop. What I do recommend, along with most in Australia, is to keep your hats on and wear long sleeves in the surf. And find joy and love in the shade!

TEENAGERS AND HORMONES

Whether we are going through our teenage years or about to hit 'that time of the month' – it can be a rollercoaster for our skin! Many get disheartened when the first little spot shows up and, unfortunately, I know many who make a fatal mistake when this happens.

The general thing that especially young females do (but also many young men!) is they purchase a foundation to cover up their spots; unaware that most foundations (not all) are created with paraffin wax, which is made from the black wax left over when petrol is being derived from the ground. This paraffin wax is then bleached until it is white and used in many make-up products. Although it gives some quick cover up and relief, it unfortunately also damages the skin and its natural balance, to the point that over time the skin may deteriorate and get worse.

My best advice for anyone who is experiencing spots and hormonal changes in their body is to use natural products to deal with their spots. Lemon myrtle has anti-bacterial properties, for example, and activated coconut charcoal absorbs infection. You will find the recipes Anti-bacterial Face Oil (page 109) and Spot Treatment (page 111) in this book.

If the hormones are especially bad, consider trying natural remedies such as chaste tree berries to achieve more balance in your body.

Face

It is so important to look after your face – it is often exposed to a lot of sun, which is damaging, and make-up, which can cause adverse reactions. My tip is to always do less: you do not need a five-product skincare routine every morning and night. For most cases let your skin dictate what you need.

BAD HABITS

If you are someone who washes your face persistently every morning, using many products which may have harmful chemicals, you will most likely experience dry skin, combination skin or oily skin. Most people believe that these are all completely different topics when in fact they all have the same issue in common; your skin has lost its ability to produce healthy oil due to what you are putting on it (or how often you are washing it).

If you have ever discussed the topic of washing your hair with shampoo, you will meet people whose scalp becomes oily after one or two days if that is generally how often they wash their hair. Others, who only wash their hair once a week, can go an entire week without their hair being oily.

The reason for this is that when you wash your hair you are also washing off the natural oil created by your skin to protect it and keep it moisturised. This sends a signal to the skin that it needs to create more oil more often to keep up with the washing.

The same thing goes for your skin. If you are washing it daily, the skin will either not be able to create enough oil to keep it moisturised, resulting in dry skin, or it will make too much oil in your skin so it looks oily.

My best advice is to use oil-based ingredients to clean your make-up off if needed, wash as little as possible and minimise the products you use unless they are natural and organic.

These are my best tips for getting your skin balance restored:

Dry skin

If you find that your face is especially dry, try and use a more moisturising carrier oil for your face such as almond oil or macadamia oil.

Combination skin

Use jojoba, which helps the balance of your natural oil production to create a more consistent and natural production of oil in your skin.

Oily skin

Use rosehip oil, which is the driest oil of them all – it will still absorb into your skin, but it will slow down your natural oil production to create a healthier balance in your skin.

Spots and acne

Use natural remedies such as lemon myrtle (anti-bacterial), clay and activated coconut charcoal (absorbs infection).

No glow

You can drink gotu kola – a perennial plant which has natural collagen – to restore your glow and also the health of your nails and hair!

NATURAL BALANCING & ANTI-BACTERIAL FACE OIL

A gentle oil to soothe your skin while helping balance your oil production. This combination has natural anti-bacterial properties to keep spots at bay!

What you need

- 30ml glass bottle with dropper
- 10ml organic hemp oil
- 20ml organic jojoba
- 1 drop organic lemon myrtle essential oil
- 1 drop of naturally derived vitamin E (optional)

Skin and hair care

Directions

Add all of the ingredients into your bottle and give it a light shake.

Usage

Use once a day to help balance your skin's natural oil production and eliminate bacteria in your skin. Ensure you do not get it in your eyes as lemon myrtle can sting like soap.

Storage

Store in your bathroom and keep away from direct sunlight. Your oil should last you several months (without the naturally derived vitamin E), or up to two years if you add the vitamin E. If it goes rancid it will smell off and you should discard the oil.

NATURAL RECIPE SPOT TREATMENT FOR PIMPLES

A natural yet powerful paste to add directly to pimples to help kill infection while absorbing and drying the area out.

What you need

- ❧ 1 small jar for storage
- ❧ 1 tbsp charcoal
- ❧ 1 tbsp dried lemon myrtle
- ❧ 1 tbsp green Australian clay
- ❧ Organic tea tree water

Skin and hair care

Directions

Mix the powders together (do not add tea tree water to this mix yet) and store in an airtight container.

As required, take 1 teaspoon of the mixed powders and blend it with a few drops of organic tea tree water until it forms a thick paste.

Usage

Apply to your spot and let it dry completely before washing off with soap. Don't let it sit longer than 20 minutes.

Storage

Store the powder mix in an airtight container ready for use whenever you start seeing a spot develop. This powder will not go rancid and can be stored for years.

ORGANIC FACE MIST RECIPE

Face mists can be used to hydrate your skin and can contain different vitamins depending on the hydrosols used (see pages 21 and 97 for more on hydrosols). I like to keep it in my bag throughout summer for when I just need a quick pick-me-up on a hot day.

What you need

- ❧ 100ml spray bottle (amber)
- ❧ 50ml organic lavender hydrosol
- ❧ 50ml organic rose hydrosol

Directions

Pour the hydrosols in the bottle and shake lightly.

Usage

Spray on your face on a hot day, after a yoga class or sweaty activity, or just as a refresher when you need it!

Storage

Your face mist should last you up to a year when stored away from direct sunshine.

ORGANIC ANTI-BACTERIAL FACE TONER

This face toner is great if you are experiencing outbreaks or acne – the toner will work as a natural anti-bacterial spray and close your pores as well.

What you need

- 100ml spray bottle
- 20ml organic eucalyptus hydrosol
- 40ml organic tea tree hydrosol
- 40ml organic witch hazel (containing no more than 10% alcohol)

Directions

Pour all the ingredients into your bottle and shake gently.

Usage

Spray in the morning and evening before applying your normal face moisturiser.

Storage

This product should last up to one year stored away from direct sunshine.

ORGANIC REJUVENATING FACE OIL

A face oil that fits all! It should help rebalance natural oil production in your skin, so whether your skin is dry or oily this face oil is perfect either way. I really enjoy that it is fast absorbent and does not leave your face shiny after applying. It also contains a ton of vitamins for your skin, giving you a gorgeous complexion, where rosehip has natural rejuvenating properties that may just leave you looking younger for longer.

116

What you need

- 🌱 30ml bottle with dropper
- 🌱 10ml organic rosehip oil (cold pressed)
- 🌱 20ml organic jojoba oil (cold pressed)
- 🌱 1 drop lavender essential oil
- 🌱 1 drop rose geranium essential oil
- 🌱 1 drop ylang ylang essential oil
- 🌱 1 drop of naturally derived vitamin E

Directions

Pour all the ingredients into the bottle and give it a gentle shake.

Usage

Add a few drops of the oil to your face every morning or evening.

Storage

This face oil should last you up to one year stored away from direct sunlight.

Skin and hair care

Body

Our bodies are important and keeping a good and healthy diet as well as regular exercise is beneficial for us all. As with anything, we also like to keep our skin glowing and ready for summer days in our swimwear.

I can be quite lazy when it comes to looking after my body – raising three children while running a business does not leave a lot of time for regular exercise and pampering! I do, however, stock up on some good and easy to use products that I keep in my shower and on a shelf in the bathroom for my weekly routine. Yes, you can totally do this daily, but as I said, I can be quite lazy!

Skin and hair care

CELLULITE

Although skincare products won't get rid of your cellulite entirely – you will have to do some exercises for that if you are really keen – you can take the easy way (like me) to have glowing skin by using scrubs to get the blood flow going and scrape away dead skin cells in the process. I adore using coffee in my scrubs because it really kickstarts the blood flow as the skin absorbs the caffeine and it will leave your skin soft and glowing. See page 121 for a recipe suggestion.

DRY SKIN

During winter – or heck even summertime – we can get dry skin as the weather changes. I find that I especially get dry skin on my legs after shaving them, as well as my hands from frequently washing. You could use plain oil or even coconut oil in these cases (as the skin on your body tends to not be as sensitive as your face), however I find the consistency a little too oily and clogging, so I prefer to give it a bit of a mix and whip it up into body butter – see recipe page 124.

GLOWING SKIN

Gotu kola is my go-to tea to sip on for good collagen. Another ingredient that is highly beneficial is turmeric, so get some curries going to really get your skin glowing! My other trick is to add some cocoa powder to your body butter, which will leave your skin with a beautiful slight tan colour – great for flashing your legs in summertime.

120

From Earth

FIRMING AND EXFOLIATING BODY SCRUB

I know that personally, I might just pop out of a hot shower and sometimes scratch my skin if I feel itchy (usually from mosquito bites). I find that the skin then releases dead skin cells. This is a natural process we all go through as our skin continuously produces new skin cells and leaves the old skin cells on top of our skin – and nothing is better than to just exfoliate these away! There are many ways you can exfoliate your skin: you can use soap bags, buy natural exfoliating soaps or you can just whip up your own natural body scrub! This is my recipe, but you can tweak it any way you like, which is the wonderful thing about scrubs.

What you need

- 4 cups of sea salt
- 2 cups organic coconut oil
- 1 cup organic jojoba oil
- 2 tbsp ground organic coffee
- 1 tbsp pink French clay
- 5ml cinnamon essential oil
- 5ml vanilla extract
- 3ml sweet orange essential oil

Directions

Melt the coconut oil in a double boiler or over a hot water bath (boil water in a large pot and melt the coconut oil in smaller pot sitting on top of the water, without the water tipping into the smaller pot).

Pour the melted oil over the salt in a bowl and mix well. Add the remaining ingredients and mix. Pour into a container of your choice.

Usage

Always ensure when using it that your body is already wet in the shower or bath as the salt won't dilute otherwise.

From Earth

Scrub with water all over your body and rinse off. Your skin should feel soft and moisturised after.

Storage
Keep away from direct sunlight and store in a cool spot. Will last up to two years.

Tip: Salts can be purchased in fine and flossy so use what you feel is best in terms of how sensitive your skin is and how harsh you want the scrub to be. Remember to always use a scrub on wet skin as the salt will not dilute otherwise and it will scratch your skin instead.

Skin and hair care

LUSH BODY BUTTER

Body butter looks just like whipped cream – and almost good enough to eat! It is made up of oils and butter and will moisturise your skin deeply. I would not advise using this on your face but instead use it on your body and dried hands and feet – you will feel amazing afterwards!

What you need

- 2 cups organic shea butter
- 1 cup organic coconut oil
- 1 tsp candelilla wax
- 50ml organic jojoba oil
- 1 drop of natural vitamin E

124

Optional:

- ❧ 10 drops lavender essential oil

- ❧ 10 drops grapefruit essential oil

- ❧ 5 drops rose geranium essential oil

You can create your own essential oil blend for this mix.

Directions

In a double boiler or over a hot water bath (boil water in a large pot and melt the ingredients in a smaller pot sitting on top of the water), melt your shea butter, coconut

Skin and hair care

oil and candelilla wax until it is all completed melted. Pour into a container and let it sit until the next day.

Once the oils have become a solid form again, put it into a bowl and add the jojoba oil. Start whisking it with an electric mixer – more jojoba can be added if you find that the consistency is too solid. Once it starts to form little peaks, add your essential oils and vitamin E and whisk again. Pour into a container and keep it in a cool place away from direct sunlight.

Usage
Warm the butter up in your hands by rubbing them together, then rub all over your body. Not suitable for the face.

Storage
Will store well for up to two years.

Hair

My children, you might be shocked to learn, have never had their hair washed with shampoo. Yet you will not find anyone with more gorgeous hair than my children! I am not saying don't ever bathe or wash your children, I am just making a point that you don't necessarily need a commercial shampoo (that is generally loaded with chemicals).

You might be wondering how this can be the case.. Let me explain. Your scalp, like any animal's, will create natural oil to protect you, with just enough of what you need. If you, however, wash it off daily with shampoo, your scalp will go into overproduction of oil, which will make your scalp oily after a day or two.

So, if you want to try a more natural way of looking after your hair, these are my tips:

- Try and detox; opt for going one day extra than you normally would in between using shampoo, and let your scalp get used to producing less oil. It will be a lot better for your hair and scalp.

- If you have not tried using a shampoo bar yet, I highly recommend it! They are great for the planet (no plastic container!), gentle on your hair and more natural than regular shampoo is. They still lather wonderfully!

- Create your own hair treatment (recipe below) when your ends need some nourishment.

Skin and hair care

NATURAL HAIR TREATMENT

If you find that your ends are dry and cracked – don't grab your scissors just yet! Instead try and use this wonderful hair balm on your ends.

What you need

- 🌿 1 jar to keep your hair treatment in
- 🌿 100ml organic coconut oil
- 🌿 1 tbsp castor oil
- 🌿 1 tbsp argan oil
- 🌿 1 tsp rosemary essential oil

130

From Earth

Directions

First ensure that the coconut oil is not too cold, as it otherwise won't mix well. You can use a hair dryer to warm it up a bit first if you need to. Whisk all the ingredients together and pour into your jar. Leave in your jar until it has set, or pop it in your fridge if the room is too hot.

Usage

Use around a tablespoon of the treatment for long hair, less if it's short, and warm it up in your hands by rubbing them together. Run it through your hair, concentrating on the ends and avoiding the roots. Leave it in for 30 minutes and wash out using shampoo. You will look like you just came from the hairdresser!

Storage

Needs to be stored below room temperature, and away from direct sunlight. Can be stored in your fridge or a cold cupboard.

Skin and hair care

NATURAL SALTY HAIR SPRAY

If you are like me and you love the beautiful texture the ocean gives to your hair – but cannot always jump in the water – this is an easy way to make your own salt spray to get the look!

What you need

- 100ml amber bottle with spray cap
- 2 tbsp sea salt
- 100ml water

Directions

Boil the water in a pot with the salt until the salt has completely dissolved. Leave it to cool down until it is room temperature. Pour it into your bottle and it's ready.

Usage

Spray into wet or dry hair from 30cm away.

Storage

This blend will only last one month before it goes rancid. But it is quick and easy to make a new batch – you can just empty your bottle, clean it with mineral water and pour the fresh mix in.

> Tip: *Always store a bottle of argan oil with a few drops of rosemary essential oil in your bathroom – this is perfect for dry hair and split ends and will strengthen your hair.*

Skin and hair care

Babies and Family

Anyone who has already gone through parenthood will tell you – there is nothing more obsessive than a new parent looking to find the absolute best for their new baby! The stress we put ourselves through trying to be perfect and do the right things is tremendous – throw into that equation that there are about a million different pieces of advice for mums out there and it can be so hard to navigate and decide what is right for you and your baby! It is simply a learning experience where you listen to advice but most importantly follow your instinct; you are born to be a mum and no matter what you will be a good one if you are already thinking about what's best for your baby!

My instincts really kicked in when I had children and, after three of them, I am still not always sure I am doing the right things. These are my tips and what I have learned on how to look after my skin through my pregnancy and how to look after my babies' skin. Take or leave as it suits you.

PREGNANCY

Going through pregnancy can be a blissful time for some people – but it can certainly also be an absolute emotional rollercoaster that makes you so sick that you don't ever want to go through it again! Throw in all the body changes and stretchmarks and we really have a lot to adjust to, for better or worse.

PREGNANCY BODY OIL

A moisturising body oil – to improve the elasticity of your skin to protect it and help it to adjust to the changes it is going through.

What you need

- 100ml bottle with pump (amber)
- 60ml organic hemp oil
- 30ml organic rosehip oil
- 10ml organic jojoba oil
- A few drops of organic lavender essential oil (optional)

Directions

Pour all the ingredients into a bottle and shake gently.

Usage

Rub over your belly after every shower to replenish your skin and its elasticity.

Storage

Keep away from direct sunlight and store in a cool spot.

From Earth

BABIES

Babies are born with a natural immune system on their skin, protecting them from getting sick once they are born. Due to this, my advice is to not give them a bath in the early stages. Instead, use a cloth soaked with lukewarm water to clean them when they are dirty. This way you protect their skin as much as possible.

When my eldest daughter was born, I was determined to set a good example and put her in a good routine following books of guidance and advice. At the time most books recommended giving your baby a bath every night before sleep time to calm them down. This was the worst thing I have ever done and I regretted doing it long after. She ended up with a really bad case of eczema due to her skin drying out from all the baths and, while we received advice from the doctors as to what creams to use, they were filled with chemicals and ingredients so bad I could not even use it on her face. Instead I stopped the bathing and used my own Natural Eczema Relief (page 150) on her eczema. Her skin cleared within three days and she has never had a bad flare up since.

Skin and hair care

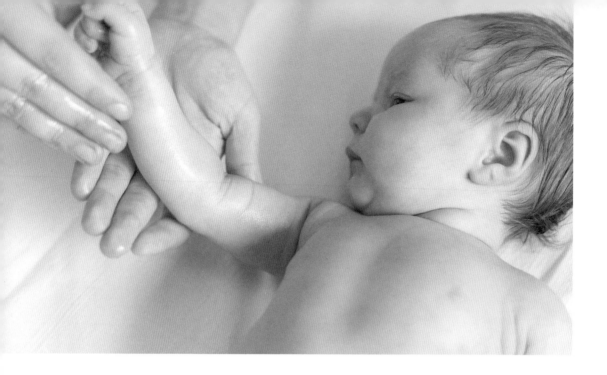

BABY NOURISHING OIL

My advice is to not use creams that have a lot of man-made preservatives on babies. There is no point using these unnatural ingredients when you can easily whip up something 100% natural that is great for your baby's skin.

What you need

- 100ml bottle with pump
- 80ml organic jojoba oil
- 20ml organic hemp oil
- 3 drops of organic lavender essential oil

138

Directions

Pour all ingredients into your bottle and shake gently.

Usage

Rub over your baby's skin when it is dry or after giving your baby a bath or wash.

Storage

This oil will last up to one year if stored away from direct sunlight in a cool spot.

Tip: Natural organic castor oil works as a waterproof thick moisturising layer on your baby's skin and is perfect for red noses or red bums.

Remedies

Stress and Anxiety

Before I start this section on stress and anxiety, I want to make it clear: if you are persistently experiencing skincare issues please see a professional as it could be related to your diet or a medical condition. However, if you are not going through your teenage years but your skin, from time to time, 'flares up', it could potentially be due to going through a stressful time in your life (or of course, it could just be that time of the month). Stress and anxiety really sneak up on you – you might be super stressed at work, or you could be going through an emotional time, and all of a sudden there is a cold sore or a pimple on the worst possible spot!

What you want to do first of all is try to relax: do some meditation, go for a walk or whatever works for you to de-stress. For me personally I'll grab a 500-piece puzzle and pop some Dire Straits in the music player. But I also have a few recipes to help me with cold sores and to help relax myself.

NATURAL COLD SORE REMEDY

This natural oil blend will help reduce the swelling of your cold sore and, if used before it 'erupts', you might find that it never does. It has been a life saver for me every time I am doing an expo with my business as a cold sore always sneaks up on me when I work many hours a day and don't have time to stop.

What you need

- 10ml roll-on bottle
- 9ml organic castor oil
- 3 drops lemongrass essential oil
- 3 drops lemon myrtle essential oil

Directions

Fill your bottle with castor oil and add the essential oils.

Usage

Use as you would a lip gloss and roll onto your lips over the cold sore.

Warning

Please be aware, this will sting your lips and you might want to apply some natural lip balm or plain castor oil afterwards to ease the sting. This stinging feeling is telling you that it is working. Just be careful not to rub it anywhere else!

Storage

Will store for up to one year; keep away from direct sunlight.

NATURAL RELAX AND DE-STRESS OIL

I love blending carrier oils with essential oils so that I can apply them straight to my skin without the essential oils 'burning' me. They are super easy to make and you can get really creative with your preferred ingredients, using any essential oil you like! This recipe is designed to relax your mind and de-stress you.

What you need

- 10ml roll-on bottle
- 8ml organic jojoba oil (can be substituted with almond, rosehip or other liquid carrier oils)
- 3 drops lavender essential oil
- 2 drops rosemary essential oil
- 1 drop sweet orange essential oil
- 1 drop lemon essential oil

Directions

Add the oils into your roll-on bottle and gently shake to combine.

Usage

Roll onto your pulse points – temples, neck and wrists – when you need to unwind.

Storage

Keep away from direct sun. Should last up to 12 months.

Tip: this blend may also help with insomnia or sleep issues.

RELAXING BATH SALTS

Pop the music on, grab yourself a glass of wine or hot cup of tea as you prepare yourself
to relax and indulge in a hot bath.

What you need

- 2 cups sea salt
- 2 cups Epsom salt
- 2 tsp green or red clay
- 5ml lavender essential oil
- 5ml rosemary essential oil

Optional: – add as many of these
dried botanicals as you like:

- Organic dried rose petals
- Organic dried calendula flowers
- Organic dried lavender flowers
- Organic dried chamomile flowers

146

From Earth

Directions

Mix it all together and store in an airtight container.

Usage

Use four or five tablespoons of the mixture each time you have your own quiet bath time.

Storage

Ensure that your salts are stored in a completely airtight container, or they will lose their scent. The essential oils will go rancid after around twelve months. Store in a dark, cool spot away from direct sunlight.

Eczema and Psoriasis

There are so many people with eczema and many people are not even aware that this is what they are suffering from. Eczema is unfortunately a lifelong skin condition that can be managed but may flare up from time to time. Some people, however, experience severe cases of eczema to the point that they are in constant pain and uncomfortable itchiness. It is literally like having a massive mosquito bite that you just want to itch – but when you do it is sometimes quite painful.

I have learned a lot about eczema from people suffering severely who, together with my daughter, helped inspire me to develop my natural remedies. Here are some of the things I have learned:

- Eczema thrives on heat! Do not let your children have too many blankets and don't put too many layers on yourself.

- Hot showers are a no no! Same with hot baths. That itchiness will come creeping in quickly. Water tends to dry out the skin when you have eczema, as it washes off your natural oil protection layer, and the heat will make the eczema flare up into a full sized rash quickly.

- Avoid coconut oil. I have heard many people say that they found this or that article on coconut oil and that it is great for eczema. It is true that coconut has many incredible properties; however, it is a very fatty oil! This means that it will clog your pores, not allowing your skin to breathe, which will result in your eczema getting even more itchy! So, use oils that are non-clogging.

- Diet is important. I am not a specialist on diets, but I know that personally I was diagnosed with gestational diabetes, and later as a coeliac, so no, my inners are clearly not too happy! Sugar is one thing that will irritate and flare up your organs, so ensure you don't eat too much sugar. If you feel that you are frequently bloated, tired, or otherwise something is bothering you, do consult with a specialist and ensure that you are not lacking vitamins or suffering from any other conditions or intolerances.

NATURAL ECZEMA RELIEF

If you really want something soothing to reduce your rash, this is the oil you need to make for yourself. It is a strong anti-inflammatory oil which will soothe and help heal the skin faster. It is also my top-selling oil that everyone keeps coming back for! For the first time ever I am sharing my secret recipe with you.

What you need

- A large bottle with lid
- A smaller bottle, preferably with a pump insert or dropper
- Organic hemp oil
- Dried organic calendula flowers
- Dried organic nettle leaf
- Dried organic marshmallow root
- 1-2 drops naturally derived vitamin E

From Earth

- ☙ 2 drops of lavender essential oil
- ☙ Clean cotton cloth
- ☙ A jug

Directions

Fill your large bottle with 1/3 calendula flowers, 1/3 nettle leaf and 1/3 marshmallow root. Fill the organic hemp oil to the top to cover all the dried botanicals. Put the lid on and let it sit for 3-4 weeks to really get the nutrients and benefits infused into the oil.

Once it has been sitting for 3-4 weeks, use a clean cotton cloth to strain the oil through into a jug, making sure the botanicals stay in the cloth, then squeeze as much oil out of it as you can. Once you have all the oil, add 1-2 drops of your natural vitamin E, mix well, and add the lavender. Finally, pour the solution into the smaller bottle.

Usage

Add straight onto your eczema, psoriasis or other skin rash – it's safe for the face as well.

Storage

Store in a cool, dark space for up to two years. Keep away from direct sunlight.

Sore Throat

When it's that time of the year and you feel your throat is getting sore, besides a hot shower, blankets and a good movie this is my go-to remedy tea to feel immediate relief.

ORGANIC SORE THROAT TEA

This soothing tea will help as a natural anti-inflammatory, while the liquorice will help with any throat pain.

What you need

- 2 cups organic liquorice root
- 2 cups organic chamomile
- 1 cup organic cinnamon
- 1 cup organic ginger
- ½ cup organic nettle

Directions

Blend the ingredients together and store in an airtight jar for use when needed.

Usage

Add a tablespoon of the blend to a pot, or a teaspoon full to a strainer, and leave for minimum five minutes.

Storage

Store in an airtight container away from direct sunlight – will store up to three years.

Tip: *Add fresh cut lemon and honey to your tea.*

From Earth

Runny Nose

Your nose keeps running, you get red all around it, it hurts and blocks your airways …
Here is what I do when the kids or I need to get better quick!

ORGANIC VAPOUR ESSENTIAL OIL

This little bottle is essential in your natural apothecary cabinet. You can add drops of this
to your shower, bath, diffuser or roll on.

What you need

- 🌿 15ml amber or dark bottle with dropper
- 🌿 5ml peppermint essential oil
- 🌿 5ml eucalyptus essential oil
- 🌿 5ml rosemary

Directions

Add the ingredients to your bottle and shake gently.

Usage

Boil some water and drop in a few drops of this oil. Breathe in the steam with a towel over your head – it will help clear your nose and let you breathe again. You can also drop a few drops in your shower or bath.

Warning

Avoid getting any direct contact with the skin and especially the eyes!

Storage

Store away from direct sunlight for up to two years.

VAPOUR ROLL ON

What you need

- 10ml roll on bottle
- 5ml organic castor oil
- 5ml organic jojoba oil
- Vapour essential oil blend (see page 155)

Directions

Add the castor oil and jojoba to your bottle and add 5 drops of the vapour essential oil blend. Shake gently.

Usage

Roll on around the chest, nose and throat.

Warning

Avoid getting this oil near your eyes!

Storage

Store away from direct sunlight. Will last up to 12 months.

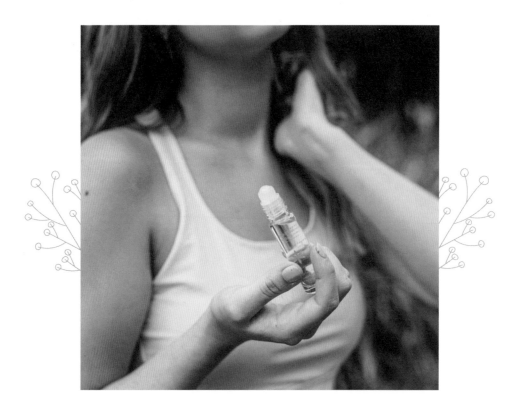

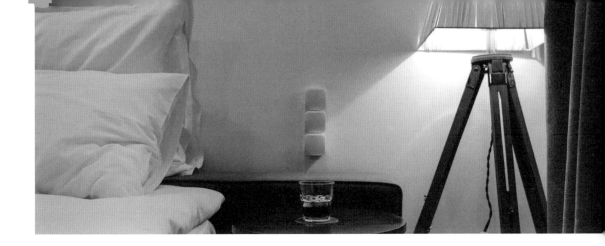

Insomnia

Unfortunately, this can be a common issue for some people. This is the recipe I have created to help my clients. It is delicious and perfect to sip on before going to bed.

ORGANIC SLEEP BETTER TEA

I have a terrible habit of drinking coffee, even in the evening, and it means that my brain will just not relax and go to sleep. So, I have substituted my bad habit for my delicious tea habit, which calms me down and relaxes my mind. The valerian root is not always loved by all, but this blend creates a nice flavour while the valerian root is proven to help with insomnia.

What you need

- 2 cups organic valerian root
- 2 cups organic cinnamon
- 1 cup organic liquorice root
- 1 cup organic nettle
- 1 cup organic chamomile

- 1 cup roasted organic dandelion root
- 1 cup organic verbena
- 1 cup organic lavender
- ¼ cup organic catnip

Directions
Blend all of the herbs together in a bowl.

Usage
Use two tablespoons for a pot or a teaspoon for a cup.

Storage
Store in an airtight container away from direct sunlight.

160

ORGANIC SPICY VALERIAN ROOT LATTE

Tastes like the most delicious chai and is my go-to for my nightly drink. I mix it up with warm coconut milk and maple syrup. Perfect to help relax your mind at the end of the day.

What you need

- ❧ 2 cups organic ground valerian root powder
- ❧ 1 ½ cups organic cinnamon powder
- ❧ 1 cup organic roasted dandelion root powder
- ❧ ½ cup organic cardamom powder
- ❧ ½ cup organic ginger powder
- ❧ ¼ cup organic black pepper powder
- ❧ 1 tsp organic cayenne powder (use less or more depending how spicy you like it)

Directions

Blend all the powders together.

Usage

Use one tablespoon for one cup of hot milk of your choice. I personally love to use organic coconut milk, which you should be able to find in most supermarkets. Add a dash of maple syrup to taste. Enjoy!

Storage

Use an airtight container to keep it stored for longer. Will store well for up to two years.

ORGANIC SLEEP MIST

Spray it on your linen or your face and lie down to relax!

What you need

- 🌿 100ml spray bottle
- 🌿 50ml organic lavender hydrosol
- 🌿 50ml organic rosemary hydrosol

Directions

Pour into your bottle and shake gently.

Usage

Spray from around 30cm away from your face when you need a pick-me-up, or spray directly onto linen.

Storage

Will store for up to one year away from direct sunlight.

From Earth

Headaches

Tension and headaches are some of the absolute worst! It's hard to concentrate or get on with doing anything when it really kicks in, so here are my top recipes to help deal with it better, naturally.

Tip: I recommend using peppermint or lavender essential oil blended with a carrier oil to create a roll on to apply to temples when you are experiencing a headache.

ORGANIC TEA FOR TENSION AND HEADACHES

Great to keep in the medicine cupboard to grab whenever the headache sets in!

What you need

- 2 cups organic lavender
- 1 cup organic peppermint
- 1 cup organic elderflower
- ½ cup organic skullcap

Directions

Mix all the dried ingredients together.

Usage

Use two tablespoons for a pot or one teaspoon for a cup. Leave it to sit for five minutes.

Storage

Store in an airtight container away from direct sunlight.

Muscle Pain

There is nothing better than a good exercise to get you going and make you feel better – but sometimes when the exercise has been a bit intense you may feel pain kicking in over the next few days. Here is how I deal with it.

ORGANIC MUSCLE RELAXANT BODY BUTTER

A glorious moisturiser and perfect to massage with. Use this whipped cream when pain kicks in to give you some relief.

What you need

- 2 cups organic shea butter
- 1 cup organic coconut oil
- 1 tsp candelilla wax
- 50ml organic jojoba oil
- 10 drops wintergreen essential oil
- 10 drops camphor essential oil
- 10 drops peppermint essential oil
- 4 drops naturally derived vitamin E

Directions

In a double boiler or over a hot water bath (a large pot of boiling water with a smaller bowl placed in the water), melt your shea butter, coconut oil and candelilla wax until it is all completely melted. Pour into a container and let it sit until the next day.

Once the oils have become a solid form again, put it into a bowl and add the jojoba oil. Start whisking it with an electric mixer – more jojoba can be added if you find that the consistency is too solid. Once it starts to form little peaks, add your essential oil and vitamin E and whisk again. Pour into a container.

Usage

Avoid using on the face. Rub onto back, arms and legs where your muscles are sore and gently massage while rubbing it in.

Storage

Keep it below room temperature and away from direct sunlight. Will store well for up to two years.

From Earth

Period Pain

Every time my period rolls around I believe (like many other women) that I may be experiencing some of the worst period pain in history. I remember people telling me, well just wait until you have kids and, honestly, the majority of the time I was going through the birthing of my children I had the same pain levels as some of my periods! It can be super painful and enough to force us to just lie down. Before you grab your painkillers try these things out to give you some relief!

LAVENDER HEAT PACK

So, I would totally love to tell you that I am great at sewing, but unfortunately it is not one of my talents. So instead, I had to get a little bit creative when I made this. It works for me, it's easy to make and gives so much relief! If you are handy with a needle, feel free to sew your own lavender heat pack using this or another filling.

What you need

Old cotton pillowcase

- 🌱 A bag of rice
- 🌱 Cotton string

Optional:

- 🌱 Dried organic lavender
- 🌱 Dried organic peppermint
- 🌱 Dried organic rose petals

Directions

Fill your pillowcase with rice (1/6 full).

Add optional organic dried lavender, peppermint and/or rose petals (I use 1 cup of each).

Roll the pillowcase into a sausage, ensuring that the rice and botanicals stay in one spot.

Tie cotton string around it, one either side and two in the middle so it does not unfold itself.

Usage

Pop it in the microwave for 40 seconds to one minute (depending on the strength of your microwave), take it out and ensure it is not so hot it will burn your skin. When you are happy with the temperature, lay it over your abdomen and relax.

Storage

Should store well and be usable for several years.

Tip: You can add other gorgeous dried botanicals such as rosemary or verbena to give it more fragrance.

TEA FOR PERIOD PAIN AND PMS

Before you reach for the aspirin or paracetamol try this easy remedy. Drink it as a tonic or as a tea to help with pain, mood swings and headaches.

What you need

- ❧ 2 cups organic peppermint tea
- ❧ 2 tbsp organic chaste tree berries
- ❧ 2 tbsp dong quai
- ❧ 2 tbsp black haw

From Earth

Directions

Blend the ingredients together and store in an airtight container.

Usage

Use two tablespoons for a pot, one teaspoon for a cup, and drink it hot as a tea. Or, store it in the fridge and have a shot every morning and night a few days before your period is due and during.

Storage

Keep in an airtight container away from direct sunlight. Will store well for up to two years.

Tip: You can spice up your tea and add other flavours by adding liquorice, cinnamon, ginger, verbena or lemon.

Stomach Pain and Digestion

Being a coeliac I have gone through a lot of stomach pain through the years. I also know so many people with digestion and inflammation issues. This remedy I've got for you is a keeper to get you cleansed and feeling better!

TUMMY SOOTHER TEA

My go-to tea for bloating and cramps! It is a natural anti-inflammatory and will soothe and heal your guts. It is also super delicious and naturally sweet.

What you need

- 2 cups organic liquorice
- 1 cup organic marshmallow root
- 1 cup organic cinnamon
- 1 cup organic chamomile
- ½ cup anise seeds
- ½ cup fennel seeds
- ¼ cup buchu leaf
- ¼ cup ginger

Directions
Blend the ingredients together.

Usage
Use two tablespoons for a pot or one teaspoon per cup. Let it sit for five minutes.

Storage
Store in an airtight container away from direct sunlight.

General house

Your house is your haven; it's where you feel like you can be you and where you enjoy your family time. Keeping a general good flow and Zen feeling in the house is what makes me feel good. Here are some of the things I like to keep around me.

Essential oils for diffusers

Diffusers are great – they send those essential oils into the air and create a beautifully scented home. If you are not keen on making candles you can still easily get creative in making your own essential oil blends!

Here are my favourite blends:

Herbal Delight
5ml lemongrass, 5ml lemon myrtle and 5ml pine

Floral Delight
5ml lavender, 5ml rose geranium and 5ml grapefruit

177

Australian Natives
5ml tea tree, 5ml eucalyptus and 5ml lemon myrtle

Refreshing Burst
4ml peppermint, 4ml eucalyptus, 4ml rosemary and 3ml pine

Musky Notes
4ml patchouli, 4ml sandalwood, 4ml ylang ylang, 4ml frankincense and 3ml grapefruit

From Earth

Keeping Insects at Bay

Insects and bugs will always find their way into your house. These are my tips to keep the ants away and mosquitos flying over to the neighbour instead!

STOP THE ANTS!

A spray to keep the ants from walking through your windowsill.

What you need

- 15ml amber bottle
- 100ml spray bottle
- Mineral water
- 10ml cinnamon essential oil
- 3ml tea tree essential oil
- 2ml rosemary essential oil

179

Directions

Pour the essential oils into your small amber bottle and shake gently. Then fill your spray bottle with mineral water to about 95% full and use 5ml of the essential oil in the bottle. Store the remaining essential oil for next fill up.

Usage

Spray the blend directly on windowsills, doors, furniture and benches to keep the ants away.

Storage

Once added to the water, this blend will only last a few weeks before going rancid. My tip is to keep the oils at hand and just make a new bottle every 2-3 weeks.

Mosquitos

The sun is setting but you want to stay outdoors to enjoy the fresh air, without getting eaten up by mosquitos. These are my tips to keep them at bay.

MOSQUITO REPELLENT ESSENTIAL OIL

This essential oil can be used in your diffuser to keep mosquitos away from the house, or you can add a few drops to a spray bottle with water – just be aware that in water it will go rancid in a few weeks, so you will need to make a new batch every now and again when needed.

What you need

- 15ml amber drop bottle
- 5ml lemon essential oil
- 5ml basil essential oil
- 5ml citronella essential oil

Directions

Pour the oils into your drop bottle and shake gently.

Usage

Use the essential oil in the organic mosquito repellent body oil (pg 183) or use in an oil diffuser.

Storage

Will last up to two years when stored away from direct sunlight.

ORGANIC MOSQUITO REPELLENT BODY OIL

A must have when camping or doing a barbeque! This oil is 100% natural and I promise you it will keep those mosquitos at bay!

What you need

- 100ml bottle with pump
- 40ml organic hemp oil
- 40ml organic almond oil
- 15ml organic castor oil
- 5ml mosquito repellent essential oil blend (pg 181)

Directions
Pour all the ingredients into your bottle and shake gently.

Usage
Use directly on your skin as a natural body oil which will keep the mosquitos away and moisturise your skin.

Storage
Will store well for up to 12 months.

From Earth

SMUDGE STICKS

I think I might have an obsession for creating smudge sticks. Even when I was a child, I would grab plants from my grandparents' garden and hang them up to dry (not knowing I could burn them later on!). Smudge sticks have been used for centuries in different cultures and for different purposes. They are believed to cleanse the energy in your home or around a person. Get creative and make your own from the plants you have foraged when outdoors!

Commonly used plants are:

- ❧ Lavender (love and healing)
- ❧ Rosemary (remembrance)
- ❧ Sage (cleansing bad energies)
- ❧ Peppermint (de-stress & aromatherapy)
- ❧ Eucalyptus (healing and cleansing)

Tip: Want to make your smudge stick especially beautiful? Try adding small, dried roses, verbena, lemon balm, gypsophila, layering rose petals around it or adding a string of dried cloves, a cinnamon stick or dried orange for fragrance.

SMUDGE STICK RECIPE

- Gather the plants you have foraged and want to use to create your smudge stick.
- Use the bulkiest items first. Create the shape by bending them if you have to.
- Start to build stick by adding in layers on top, following the shape you have outlined.
- Grab some cotton string that will burn well and start wrapping it around as tight as you can.
- Cut excess off at either end if needed.
- Hang it upside down to dry for a few weeks.
- When dry, retie the string to keep the shape as neat and close as possible.
- Ready to burn.

From Earth

Going Eco friendly and sustainable

LIVING SUSTAINABLY (ZERO WASTE)

It is amazing how so many are embracing zero waste. I see it all the time; customers coming in with their reusable takeaway cups or water bottles, shops ditching the plastic bags, customers using produce bags to buy their veggies and fruit and so on. It is so important to me to find ways to reduce plastic and allowing my family, myself, and my customers to use zero waste products. Here are some great ways to go plastic-free which I highly recommend trying!

SHAMPOO BARS

Shampoo bars are obviously plastic free – but they are also much more natural and good for your hair. There are many different variants on the market now, so don't give up if you find that the first one you try is not suitable for you and your hair. Just like any shampoo in a bottle, the scent, texture and results vary depending on the shampoo bar you buy. Go for a good quality bar that is organic, if possible, and that contains some salt, as it lathers better and cleans your hair in a more natural way. You will find options for different hair types containing different clays and essential oils, so find one that you think will suit you.

CONDITIONER BARS

Conditioner bars work just like normal conditioner, except they are made into a solid form to avoid the plastic containers. They will soften your hair and make it easier to comb through. If you find that you need volume from the scalp and want to avoid your hair looking flat, just stroke it through at the ends to give your hair moisture and make it less tangled.

From Earth

DEODORANT BARS

Deodorant bars can be tricky. Most found on the market are completely natural, however, this also means more fuss in most circumstances compared to what you might be used to. You need to rub it into your underarms and then let it dry for 5-10 minutes as they are mostly based on oil contents. Once you have found a good deodorant bar, though, there are so many benefits! They are natural, so you will not have to worry about the chemicals. Essential oils such as lemon myrtle will naturally kill the bacteria that creates bad odours, while clay contents or diatomaceous earth will help it dry more quickly. Please be aware that they may stain clothes slightly, so do not put your favourite white top on right after applying!

LOTION BARS

Lush and delicious lotion bars! They are moisturisers created in a hard shape, but once you start rubbing it into your skin they slightly soften and leave a gorgeous moisturising layer on your skin. They are not recommended for the face as the oils will mostly be based on coconut, mango or shea – meaning they have a higher fat content and may clog the delicate facial skin. However, they are perfect for legs, arms and body. They are plastic free and many of them smell amazing!

SOAP BARS

I could write a novel on soap bars and how they are created, but let's keep it simple! Go for organic, cold pressed soap with essential oils if you want the most luxurious experience, with a high-quality soap that's good for the environment too. By using soap rather than a bottled shower gel you are avoiding plastic containers, and they are handy when travelling as well. You will find a huge range of different types containing clays (try and avoid artificial colouring), oils and essential oils, so enjoy hunting for the one that is right for you.

BODY SCRUB BARS

Quite a new invention that might not be easy to find, these work just like a normal body scrub, except it is made in a handy bar shape, easy to lather into your body and scrub off dead skin cells while in the shower. Usually made with oils, wax, salt, and essential oils – and 100% natural.

GARDENING

My favourite activity in my home is to get out there and get my hands dirty! When you do it with your children it is even more rewarding. If you are into your own natural

190

From Earth

medicine and apothecary, why not start a garden as well? These are some easy-to-grow plants that you can pick and use anytime you need.

Aloe Vera

A hardy and drought-tolerant plant, it is incredibly easy to grow anywhere there is enough sun and heat. It is both decorative in the garden and works a treat when someone has a cut, a rash or a bruise. Kids especially find it so much fun whenever they have the slightest little red mark to pick some just so they can play with the gel found inside its leaves.

What to do with it: You can pick the outer leaf, one should be enough, and cut it open. Inside it has a magnificent gel-like substance which has anti-inflammatory properties and will soothe the skin. Ensure that you or your kids do not eat the actual leaves as these can be toxic, while the gel is safe. Must be used straight away as it will otherwise go dry and rancid.

Rosemary

A gorgeous, hardy plant that looks quite a bit like lavender and will grow almost anywhere! The flowers are great at attracting bees and the plants will fill your garden with their gorgeous aroma.

What to do with it: Use the fresh leaves for cooking or hang it to dry to give your house the scent of rosemary. You can create oil infusions, which you can use for cooking; or, infused in argan oil, rosemary works great for strengthening hair. I also recommend using it for smudge sticks.

192

Lavender

Lavender is such an easy and beautiful plant to grow. It attracts many bees, which is great for our environment. Lavender can be picked and added to a vase in your house or hung up to dry; either way looks beautiful.

What to do with it: Lavender is incredibly versatile and can be used for so many things. My advice is to firstly dry up the flowers and store them in a jar when they are completely dry. You can now use these for baths, oil infusions, tea, heat packs or smudge sticks – or fill a cotton bag to place in your linen drawer or under your pillow.

Peppermint

Watch out, this one behaves like a weed! It will literally take over your garden, which might be desirable if you want mint galore, but if you want to keep your garden intact and only grow a normal amount I would suggest you plant this in a pot … where it can't escape. It will literally hang over the side to try and grow roots in the ground next to its pot. Yes it is a cheeky plant, but I love it!

What to do with it: Delicious, beautiful tea that may help you with headaches and indigestion. You can throw the leaves in as they are to brew, or you can hang them upside down to dry and pick the leaves as you need them.

You can also make a mint-flavoured oil as a dressing for your salads and keep it ready to go. I love mixing some mint-infused olive oil with garlic and chilli. It looks beautiful but also tastes delicious!

Nettle

This was a hard one for me to find in the local centres as unfortunately this plant can be quite misunderstood! Nettle will give you a rash on your skin if you come into contact with the outer leaves, which can feel a little painful (especially for kids). It is also a weed so just like the peppermint it will try and take over your garden – keep it in a pot! With all of the bad things said about nettle, it is my favourite plant. If you are ever unfortunate enough to get a rash from the outer leaves, you need only to pick some leaves carefully, by grabbing the leaf from the middle and pulling it off. Scrunch it up so it doesn't sting anymore and rub it all over your rash – I guarantee you will be immediately happy!

Nettle can be used like this for any rash or skin condition, such as eczema and psoriasis. It has incredible anti-inflammatory properties and will help heal your skin quickly.

What to do with it: Pick the leaves (with gloves), scrunch them up and rub them straight onto a skin rash, mosquito bite, insect bite, eczema, psoriasis or other irritation to feel its immediate healing effect. Nettle is also great for the stomach, so while you are at it brew some tea for digestion too.

How to include the kids

GO FORAGING

Kids absolutely love getting their hands dirty and it is so easy to include them in learning about plants. Often my kids and I will go for walks and, depending on the area or neighbourhood, we may find and take little cuttings of plants such as lavender, peppermint, rosemary, eucalyptus and aloe vera.

GO TO YOUR LOCAL NURSERY!

Got inspired to do some gardening? Take the kids with you! Let them choose their own plant or seeds and let them help you out in the garden with the planting and watering. They will feel the enormous pleasure of watching their little seedlings grow into plants and perhaps into fruits or vegetables!

195

About the author

*My desire is for my children to grow up in a
less materialistic world where we can all love
our own skin and look after it naturally.*

When Charlotte Rasmussen came to Australia she found it difficult to find natural, organic skincare products and remedies similar to those she had used in her upbringing in Scandinavia. Due to her passion for teaching what she had been taught to her own three children, she created From Earth, a business that became an organic reality as others were looking for the same natural remedies.

Her aim is to re-educate others about skincare and haircare, and shed more light on natural remedies. It has been one of her biggest passions to create natural products for herself and her family, and to share them with friends, family and customers.

There is very little information on the market of our overall use of products made with natural ingredients and why they are so much better for wellbeing. Charlotte is truly grateful and honoured to have the opportunity to share the knowledge she has gained from her upbringing and study.

From her humble beginnings in her kitchen in 2017 she has now settled in the Surfcoast, Victoria, where From Earth has grown into a large business that ships products globally.

www.fromearth.com.au

From Earth

Resources

Desk Reference to Nature's Medicine by Steven Foster and Rebecca L. Johnson (National Geographic).

This book is the bible of natural medicine and it should be in everyone's cupboard! It takes you through all the continents and will teach you about the incredible botanicals that all different cultures use, as well as going into detail about what has been believed and what has been documented as fact and how.

It is easy to read, understand and follow and will give you many fun facts and stories.

What is truly inspiring about this book is how cultures for centuries have used certain plants as natural remedies long before laboratories proved them to be true to belief. It is a must-have for anyone who is passionate about natural medicine and was an enormous help in writing this book.

A Manual of Materia Medica and Pharmacology by David Marvel Reynolds Culbreth (Lea and Febiger).

This is another valuable resource for reference as it lists a wide array of organic remedies.

Wherever you are
in the world there
will be an array of
wonderful, natural
products to discover.